GREETINGS from **BATON ROUGE** *Louisiana*

Greetings from **CHATTANOOGA** *Tennessee*

GREETINGS from **COLUMBUS** OHIO

Greetings from **FARGO** NORTH DAKOTA

GREETINGS FROM *Fort* **LAUDERDALE** FLORIDA

Greetings from **Ft WORTH** *Texas*

GREETINGS from **GRAND** NEW MEX

Greetings from **JOPLIN** MISSOURI *"GATEWAY TO THE OZARK PLAYGROUNDS"*

GREETINGS FROM **KEY WEST** FLA. SOUTHERNMOST CITY IN THE UNITED STATES

Greetings from **LOS ANGELES** CALIFORNIA

Greetings from **LAR**

Utah

Greetings from **OKLAHOMA CITY**

GREETINGS from **PECOS** *Texas*

Greetings FROM **ROSWELL** N.M.

Greetings FROM **St. PAUL** *Minnesota*

GREETINGS! *from* DEEP IN THE HEART of **TEXAS!** TX35

GREETINGS FROM **TULSA** OKLAHOMA "THE OIL CAPITAL OF THE WORLD"

WISC

ROADSIDE AMERICA

Edited by Jim Heimann
Foreword by C. Ford Peatross · Introduction by Phil Patton

John Margolies

ROADSIDE AMERICA

A road trip through America's past

TASCHEN

CONTENTS

Inhalt/Sommaire

PREVIOUS SPREAD Thunderbird Restaurant Sign, Mount Carmel, Utah, 1987

OPPOSITE Trail Drive-in Theater, Amarillo, Texas, 1982

FOREWORD

C. Ford Peatross

For more than three decades, John Margolies, an explorer with a mission, has crisscrossed the continental United States with a special fervor, traveling more than 100,000 miles in search of unique and typical examples of roadside and main street architecture and design. In his thousands of original photographs and his rich collection of printed ephemera, including roadmaps, postcards, and fliers, he has documented and thus preserved the vanishing symbols of a nation that is itself always of and on the road, and ever erasing its own history.

John has been likened to Herodotus, who traveled the ancient world and recorded it for posterity. I see him as the ringmaster for what might be called the "Architecture of Hyperbole," reassuring us that the featured subjects are remarkable, respectable, and key manifestations of our national, local, and individual identities. Entrepreneurial in spirit, often employing exaggerated scale or fantastical imagery, these attractions express their creators' originality, whimsy, irreverence, and sheer chutzpah. Through John's diligence and his prescient eye we have come to appreciate, celebrate, and occasionally preserve these underdogs of our highways and byways, even as they are threatened with demolition or as the next act is being set up.

The images in *Roadside America* depict the demonstrative, not the demure. As a flame to a moth, their subjects are intended to lure the traveler from his path. Like the sirens of old, they shout for attention, yet in their making are largely anonymous. Their intent is not autobiographical but pragmatic. Their appeal is to the core of our sensibilities, whether in their placement, form, colors, lighting, symbolism, movement, and graphic or other messages. Hunger, thirst, faith, vanity, security, patriotism, comfort, and pleasure are but a few of the human needs they strive to translate into the desires of the marketplace, drawing customers into their parking lots and spaces, through their entrances and to their tills. Aided by new materials and new technologies, such as the plastic potential of reinforced concrete and the seductive flash of neon lighting, the freedom of expression evident in these works is unprecedented and as distinctively a product of America's melting pot, ingenuity, and commerce.

It is appropriate that this great documentary collection should become a featured attraction of one of the world's greatest shows (and its largest library), America's oldest federal cultural institution, the Library of Congress. Here can be found the papers, archives, and works of a who's who of architecture and design.

Above the entrance to the library's Thomas Jefferson Building, luminary Ralph Waldo Emerson is enshrined in stone in a portrait bust by Jonathan Scott Hartley. Emerson espoused that truth and beauty were to be found not only in the fine arts, but also in the commonplace, and that the exploration of "the near, the low, the common" was key to the creative development of a young nation. Few things, in fact, are more truly American, democratic, and individualistic than the roadside and main street American icons recorded by John Margolies. These images promise to endure, inspire, and inform long after the structures they represent have vanished. The great American designer Charles Eames believed that good design is an expression of purpose that recognizes and responds to a need, and is by nature ephemeral. "It may (if it is good enough) later be judged as art."

Now, in the argot of the center ring: "Ladies and gentlemen, children of all ages . . . please direct your attention to the pages ahead, with their high-flying, stupefying, rule-defying, and breathtaking images, certain to amaze, inform, and delight!"

OPPOSITE Walker Evans, Coca-Cola shack, Selma, Alabama, 1935

FOLLOWING PAGE Indian Rock Shop, Holbrook, Arizona, 2003

INTRODUCTION

Phil Patton

John Margolies always gets up early to capture blue skies. The light is beautiful and the world seems cleaner. "I love the light at that time of day; it's like golden syrup," he says. "Everything is fresh and no one is there to bother you."

Some of these mornings he remembers very specifically. For instance, one time he started to drive two hours before dawn to capture the Mother Goose Market, in Hazard, Kentucky, a round stone-clad building with egg-shaped windows topped by a 15-foot-high wood-framed goose with eyes made from automobile headlights. But this is only one moment of hundreds. If you talk to Margolies for a while, you will get used to his interjection of place names, as if he were punctuating his conversation with captions. Margolies is the first to admit to his "scoreboard mentality," and he considers each of his images to be autobiographical.

"Trail Theater, Amarillo, Texas," he will say, as if in a proclamation, or, "Harold Warp's Pioneer Village, Minden, Nebraska," with a long, drawn-out emphasis on each name. "Rockwood Motel, Klamath Falls, Oregon. Wigwam Motel, Holbrook, Arizona. Susie Q. Café, Mason City, Iowa."

The Making of John Margolies

Several decades earlier, he was a child growing up in well-off New Canaan, Connecticut. He would spend hours in the back seat of his parents' car on outings that would sometimes include a drive just east of Hartford along the Berlin Turnpike, a small part of the parkway drive that turned into a few-miles-long highway strip with many traffic lights. He would marvel at all the wonderful roadside enterprises—diners, tourist cabins, drive-in theaters, and "gas war" gas stations located along this short but intense highway strip. But his parents, he recalls, never stopped at any of them except, maybe, at one of the cheap gas stations. They were never tempted by the other roadside businesses.

Margolies would not be swayed. As soon as he turned 16 he got his driver's license, and before long he was driving in a heavily used 1948 Oldsmobile to visit all the roadside businesses his parents had driven right past: the cinemas and stores of small-town main streets, the beach resorts and boardwalks, the roadside amusements and tourist Meccas.

Once he reached the University of Pennsylvania, where he studied journalism and art history, he was on the path toward the world of architecture. He earned a bachelor's degree in 1962, after which he moved on to the Annenberg School of Communication for graduate studies. There, he took a course with Gilbert Seldes, an academic champion of American popular culture, rare for the time, and author of *7 Lively Arts*, which praised musical theater and cartoons.

After graduating in 1964 with an MA in communications, he became an assistant editor at *Architectural Record* and later program director for the Architectural League of New York, where, in 1970, he would first ignite controversy. He mounted a show of work by Morris Lapidus, the architect best known for his extravagant, Hollywood-set hotels, such as the Fontainebleau and Eden Roc in Miami Beach, which flew in the face of conventional Modernist aesthetics. Architects and critics alike were appalled. In their eyes, Lapidus was not a relevant architect. "People were horrified," he remembers. "They thought I had lost my mind."

This assault on conventional taste was followed by an article in *Progressive Architecture* in praise of the Madonna Inn in San Luis Obispo, California, the well-known garish honeymoon palace where every room is decorated by a theme: stone, redwood, and grotto rooms; the Cloud Nine room; the Victorian Gardens room; the Daisy Mae and Caveman rooms.

Conventional Taste

At the time Margolies appeared on the architecture scene, Modernism still held sway. Ornament was disdained. Independent roadside establishments had been forsaken as a result of the development of America's modern highway system and the new architecture that came along with it. With the passing of the Federal-Aid Highway Act in 1956, the federal government allocated

LEFT Thunderbeast Park, Chiloquin, Oregon, 1987

OPPOSITE Anonymous, The Big Duck, Flanders, New York, c. 1931

10 $25 billion to construct new superhighways, which would be uniform in design and allow limited access with no at-grade intersections.

These new highways bypassed old roads, leaving many of the colorful, eccentric businesses to die on the vine. The Highway Act actually prohibited service stations and commercial establishments to be built on the roadside. These conditions gave impetus to the growth of national chains that sprouted up at off-ramps. Since travelers could venture farther and more often across the country, they could avail themselves of national brand names, cleanliness, and dependability. Quirky, offbeat roadside places lost their appeal in favor of the perceived safety and hygiene of chains.

The point of the interstate highways was to keep you going, to get you where you were going as quickly as possible. For Margolies, that approach to travel was the worst thing imaginable: It was another way of not being allowed to see and stop. Journalist and news reporter Charles Kuralt pointed out that it was now possible to drive from coast to coast without ever seeing anything.

Margolies recalls: "In the late 1930s, J. Edgar Hoover, head of the Federal Bureau of Investigation and America's top crime fighter, warned that roadside motels were hotbeds of vice and lawbreaking." First lady Lady Bird Johnson lamented the ugliness of the American roadside. The architect Peter Blake condemned motels and diners in his influential 1964 book *God's Own Junkyard*.

These sentiments rang in the ears of midcentury American motorists, as well as in those of select entrepreneurs, who were dreaming of turning their small roadside businesses into large, sprawling, and uniform franchises. Shell petroleum had shown early on the way to standardization by coordinating the colors and signs for all its gas stations. Their logo-shaped lamps topped the pumps with white glass shells.

Likewise, restaurant owners knew that a familiar look assured wary travelers that the food was safe and predictable. Ray Kroc famously bought the rights to the McDonald's hamburger franchise while selling Multimixer milkshake-making machines and created a consistent merchandising behemoth. In the realm of hotels, Kemmons Wilson established Holiday Inn and franchised the brand to investors across America, who would build motels according to the company's design and service standards.

The Spirit of the Road Revived

The roots of America's relationship with the road and its architecture, however, ran much deeper and in richer soil than that of Modernist taste or the sterilized climate of the 1950s. America had been in love with the automobile and all architecture related to it. The first "motor courts" arrived in the 1920s, and miniature golf became all the rage in 1930. The first drive-in theater opened for business in Camden, New Jersey, in 1933. Drive-in restaurants attained popularity from the 1920s onward.

A visual testimonial to America's bond with the road and all its quirks was created by Franklin D. Roosevelt's New Deal. The Works Progress Administration Writer's Program produced a series of state guides and history books. More importantly, the Farm Security Administration's Photography Program, which included in its ranks acclaimed photographers such as Walker Evans, Dorothea Lange, Arthur Rothstein, John Vachon, Russell Lee, Marion Post Wolcott, and Ben Shahn, produced a collection of iconic images from across the country. These photographers appreciated popular road architecture, often snapping shots of early roadside restaurants, such as the dog-shaped building Dorothea Lange shot in 1939 in Oregon.

Other photographers of the 1930s, such as Edward Weston, also took to the roads with their cameras, creating the tradition of the road photographer—the tradition that Robert Frank, Lee Friedlander, Stephen Shore, and Jeff Brouws would later continue and Margolies would ultimately inherit. In fact, he would unknowingly revisit some of the very sites documented by Weston, one of his most luminous predecessors. "It was Super Bowl Sunday, 1979," he remembers. "I was at Mammy's Cupboard off Highway 61 near Natchez, Mississippi. I did not yet know that Edward Weston had photographed the same restaurant in 1940."

Despite the prevailing Modernist currents, the 1960s brought the works of these photographers, and the old spirit of the road, into a period of revival. Curators at the Museum of Modern Art celebrated photographers who shot the contemporary roadside, such as Lee Friedlander and William Eggleston. And in 1968—two years before Margolies mounted the Lapidus show—the Newport Harbor Art Museum in California exhibited a selection of the FSA photographers' work in a show called *Just Before the War*.

Moreover, the legend of the open road was gaining heroic overtones in literature and film. It represented an almost primal American experience. It has its basis in the move west, in the journals of Lewis and Clark and the history of Francis Parkman. The story of an automotive journey cross country became a literary genre. Duncan Hines and John Steinbeck were among the most well-known American road authors. But the most recognized road book was Jack Kerouac's *On the Road*. Published in 1957, only a year after the launch of the Interstate Highway Program, it suggested the rise of a road culture alternative to the freeways and the franchises. The manuscript took the form of the road itself; it was a 120-some-foot-long scroll of paper. About the same time that Kerouac was writing, composer John Cage and artist Robert Rauschenberg made a work of art of a mini road trip by running the inked tire of Cage's Model A Ford over a scroll of paper.

The road film genre evolved from 1934's *It Happened One Night* to *They Live by Night* in 1948. It flourished with period films in the late '60s and early '70s such as *Bonnie and Clyde*, *Thieves Like Us*, and *American Graffiti*. *The Last Picture Show*, Peter Bogdanovich's film about a rural Texas town, was shot in black-and-white tones suggesting photos by Walker Evans. It was in this spirit that Margolies's own photographic enterprise was born.

On the Road

His road trips began in the middle 1970s. For Margolies, the bland standardized culture of the corporate roadside that the interstate brought was killing the creativity and individuality of the old two-lane road culture that he loved. He saw it beginning to vanish, and realized how essential it was to record it before it was gone. Witness the title of his first book of photographs: *The End of the Road: Vanishing Highway Architecture in America*.

His goal was simple documentation. "I know almost nothing about photography," he says. He stuck with his venerable Canon cameras over the years. He used a basic, 50 mm lens almost exclusively and ASA 25 film—a slow film, as photographers call it, to obtain maximum color saturation. He never made the shift to digital.

He was a historian just as much as he was a photographer. Margolies recalls one afternoon in Hamilton, New York, in 1978 when he was photographing a Shell station. "A man came up to me and asked, 'What are you doing,

12

recording it for history?' And it would turn out that the gas pumps were being torn out the next morning. So I was recording it for history."

There was a definite pattern to the trips Margolies took. Embarking in the late spring or after Labor Day, when the families and tourists were not crowding the roads, he recounts that he would "rent the biggest, most comfortable and foam-padded American car" he could find, and tune the radio to Top 40. As he departed about a half hour after dawn, having washed all of his windshields, as he did every morning on the road to give him the clearest view, the towers of Manhattan faded in his rearview mirror. He would drive until the countryside opened up. His goal was to see towns, cities, and highways he'd never seen before. As Margolies says, his "greatest goal in life is to go everywhere and see everything." He is still trying to achieve that goal.

He devised a system for living and working out of automobiles and motel rooms. In addition to coolers for keeping the film cool, there were separate bags for bathrooms and kitchens and other necessities that he would methodically load in and out at each stop. These essentials included maps — which he neatly refolded every night to preview his next day's possibilities — his travel mug, a collapsible bed board to combat "mashed potato" mattresses, clothespins to secure the drapes for privacy, and a Fred Flintstone night light on a 20-foot extension cord to illuminate unfamiliar bathrooms. He even brought a slingshot made from two intertwined rubber bands that he had determined most effectively eradicated houseflies, which often cohabited his lodgings.

Once underway, Margolies's main constraints were weather and light. Once, rainy weather trapped him in a motel for four nights in Bedford, Pennsylvania, on the Lincoln Highway as he waited for the skies to clear. He was intent upon capturing a spectacular relic: a coffee-pot-shaped building then serving as a tavern. With the skies and sun in his favor, he came to the building only to discover a few cars parked in front. Since he insisted upon taking pictures without cars — "temporal references," he calls them — he came into the bar, explained what he was doing, and then offered to buy everyone

a drink if they would move their cars. They did, and Margolies clicked way. Mission accomplished.

John Margolies as Christopher Columbus

Snippets from one trip suggest the shape of the others. Heading across the Midwest, he was amazed by a statue of Pocahontas poking up above the cornfields in Pocahontas, Iowa. He already knew about and headed for the Corn Palace in Mitchell, South Dakota, a venerable monument to the bounty of the land, redecorated each year with ears and husks of corn. In other parts of South Dakota, he photographed small-town banks turned into bars. In Rugby, North Dakota, he took a picture of a sign marking the geographic center of North America. Near Grassy Butte, North Dakota, Margolies's car began making a troublesome noise. A not-too-nearby Ford dealer diagnosed a wheel-bearing problem and fixed it for free. In Great Falls, Montana, Margolies dropped a camera — a potential catastrophe — while shooting a streamlined bus station. But a quick shake and test roll revealed no lasting harm. In Whitefish, Montana, he photographed a railroad car turned gift shop called "the Caboose" and its annex, "the Loose Caboose."

He crossed from Idaho into Washington near the town of Opportunity. He visited the Teapot Dome Service Station, near Zillah, a 1920s creation in the shape of a teapot. In Bend, Oregon, he made a great discovery: Petersen's Rock Gardens, the construction of an eccentric man named Rasmus Petersen, who created an array of bizarre rock sculptures between 1935 and 1952. In Klamath Falls he shot the Rockwood Motel, built of petrified wood, obsidian, amethyst, and other minerals.

And so his life and adventures on the roads of America continued on and off for more than 30 years and 100,000 miles or so. There was more to see than there was of him. Eventually he would become exhausted from thousands of miles and too many nights on the road, and he would be compelled to head home.

The apartment to which he returned from these trips was decorated with signage and other ephemeral evidence that he collected on the road, including metal signs advertising long-vanished brands of soft drinks and gasoline. Historic postcards of the buildings he had found were displayed on rotating racks on his desk. Although these postcards almost always came to Margolies after he had taken the corresponding photograph, they acted as the "before" shots depicting the pristine condition of the buildings decades earlier, while the "after" shots, his own photography, showed what they looked like decades later, nearly never in as good condition as they were shown in the old postcards.

Over the decades, the postcards, along with other paper ephemera, such as antique road maps, tourist brochures, and even matchbooks, have become an important corollary collection to Margolies's photographic archive.

Margolies Gains Momentum

In 1916 Henry Ford shocked people with his declaration "History is bunk." Ford seemed like a rube and reactionary when he said it, but in a sense he was a visionary. What he meant was that history in books was limited and distorted. He urged instead the study of what we today call material culture—the objects ordinary people have made and used.

Ford collected antique buildings, including houses, barns, and shops, and put all on display at Greenfield Village in Dearborn, Michigan, in the belief, he said, that he was preserving the history of people as made by their own hands. He said, "You can read an object like a book if you know how."

14

Reading towns as well as objects was exactly what Margolies knew how to do. The 200 or so rolls of film he shot on a trip would join thousands of slides stored just like books on shelves in a sprawling library in his apartment and in two other secure locations outside the city. Margolies's study of American material culture through his creation of a vast visual record would reveal much more about the era of dying roadside attractions than words alone ever could.

Ford's sentiment was echoed by Margolies's contemporary and champion, Philip Johnson. "You cannot not know history," Johnson famously stated, in reference to Postmodernism's swing away from the aesthetic of the unornamented and cold concrete box, and back to the commercial and playful. Johnson went on to laud Margolies for his documentation of an essential but "forgotten portion of the great American architectural heritage," calling him "perhaps the leading historian in this field." The architecture critic Paul Goldberger named him "the father of an entire movement."

As Margolies gained attention and acclaim, it was becoming clear that the outrage incited by his Architectural League show in 1970 was only a point of tension within a greater era of transition. Modernism was losing ground on several fronts. The decade saw energy crises that challenged the new super-highways and the ideology of speed that they had engendered. American motorists were, in a way, forced to slow down and reconnect with the original spirit of the road.

In 1972, Robert Venturi and Denise Scott Brown published the ground-breaking work *Learning from Las Vegas*, in defense of the roadside strip—writ large in Las Vegas but found outside every American city and town—as it went back to the early days of the automobile. They were fascinated by the popular architecture that Modernists renounced. The focus was on two major types of "vernacular" architecture. The first was the "Decorated Shed," which was a simple or even mundane building, sometimes covered with sign-messages that attracted attention or with a large, decorated, and often quirky sign in front, as seen on Las Vegas casinos with their overscaled "spectaculars" along the Strip. The second was the "Duck," which was a building whose shape communicated its meaning or function, such as a coffee shop shaped like a mug or a coffee pot.

The category of "mimetic buildings" was named in honor of The Big Duck—a poultry market in Long Island housed in a giant concrete building shaped like a duck. It was a local landmark, and though it was singled out for derision by Modernists such as Peter Blake, it was well loved by the public as well as by Venturi and Scott Brown. *Learning from Las Vegas* contended that these types of popular architecture could be a source of imagery and symbolism for "high architects." But Margolies went further: "Venturi and Scott Brown said it was OK to learn from this to make the real thing. I said this *was* the real thing."

This assertion aligned Margolies not only with the nascent group of Post-modern architects and critics, but also with the wave of conservationism that was building momentum. A group called the Society for Commercial Archaeology was established in 1977 to celebrate and document roadside architecture. Soon gasoline stations and diners began to be nominated for entry into the National Register of Historic Places, the American listing of buildings proposed for preservation. Just as American popular music and folk art were being revived, so too the architecture of the roadside came in for reconsideration as well.

Anthropologists, historians of popular culture, and architects were also paying more attention to the architecture of the road. In 1979, two of Venturi and Scott Brown's colleagues, Paul Hirschorn and Steven Izenour, published a book called *White Towers*, which looked at the architecture of a standardized hamburger chain. The same year Richard J. S. Gutman published the seminal *American Diner*, the first book on the history of this building type, and Warren Belasco released *Americans on the Road: From Autocamp to Motel*, a study of U.S. automobile travel from 1910 to 1945. One year later Jim Heimann presented a rich array of mimetic buildings in *California Crazy*. In 1982 John Baeder's *Gas, Food and Lodging* mingled postcards with his exacting paintings of roadside diners. In 1985 Chester Liebs published an authoritative history of 20th-century American roadside vernacular architecture, *Main Street to Miracle Mile*.

Meanwhile, Margolies continued to move toward the center of attention. The Guggenheim Fellowship in architectural criticism in 1978 was one of the first major funding sources for his work, followed by numerous grants from the National Endowment for the Arts, and in 2003 a major fellowship in photojournalism from the Alicia Patterson Foundation. These and other grants from various sources, both public and private, allowed him to continue to take extended road trips. He calculates that in 1979 and 1980 he spent four months a year, one of every three nights, in a strange motel in a place he'd never been before.

In 1980, Margolies mounted a major show of the hotels of the Catskill Mountains region of New York state, sometimes derided as the "Borscht Belt," at the Cooper-Hewitt Museum of Design in New York City. The next year, curator Richard Koshalek of the Hudson River Museum in Yonkers, New York, acknowledged the importance of his work in an exhibition called *The End of the Road*. The images in *The End of the Road* offer varying relics of roadside commerce. One elaborate neon cafe sign displayed an idealized waitress bearing a pristine milkshake in front of a verdant fir forest. There are many exteriors of the backs of drive-in movie screens sometimes enhanced by murals, whose images faded to the soft tones of fresco. The photos seemed elegiac—in the wake of the 1970s, as these roadside buildings and attractions were already beginning to fade and fall.

Margolies's images spread from museum walls to published volumes as the decade progressed. In 1987, he collected his photos of miniature golf courses for a history of the sport by Nina Garfinkel and Maria Reidelbach. The book was cleverly covered in the same Astroturf used on the courses themselves. In *Hitting the Road: The Art of the American Road Map*, he collaborated with a fellow map collector, Douglas A. Yorke Jr., and the designer Eric Baker. Under the title *Ticket to Paradise*, Margolies, in collaboration with Emily Gwathmey, assembled his photographs of movie theaters in small and larger American towns, Bijous and Odeons on often-derelict main streets. These books about small-town America allowed Margolies to sustain and advance a global awareness of such places.

Legacy

Margolies's work, which has brought him acclaim around the world, brings life to an era in American history otherwise threatened with extinction. With a perhaps ironic lack of immediate emotional pleading in their framing and viewpoint, his photographs have a heightened effect on their audience. Their direct posture and lack of visual rhetoric have deepened their impact over time. The images present all the wear and fading without romanticizing them. As his subjects have vanished, their presence in these photos has magically grown. His work depicts many structures that no longer exist except in the

LEFT Mammy's Cupboard, Natchez, Mississippi, 1979

FAR LEFT Edward Weston, Mammy, Natchez, Mississippi, 1941

OPPOSITE Mason City Tent and Awning Co., Mason City, Iowa, 1980

FOLLOWING SPREAD Club Cafe, Santa Rosa, New Mexico, 1987

16

photographs. With time, his photographs have come to contain their own reality, a mythical landscape some of us have actually inhabited but all of us imagined.

Thanks to the power of his works, Margolies has not only found acclaim in America, but also in corners of the world a long way from his home. In 2004 he was lauded by the Photographers Association of Macau. In 2009, when he had an exhibition in Rome, Italian television interviewed him as if he were a fashion celebrity.

In showing this America, Margolies has enlightened people and inspired some to become preservation advocates. He has demonstrated an uncanny instinct for arriving just ahead of the wrecking ball, which, since the publication of his work, has compelled viewers to be proactive preservationists.

Margolies's archive, as well as his collection of ephemera, has increasingly been recognized as a priceless resource in recent years. C. Ford Peatross, director of the Center for Architecture, Design and Engineering in the Prints and Photographs Division of the Library of Congress, saw the importance of his photographs and set in motion efforts to acquire them for the library—and therefore for the American people.

Peatross was not the only one to value the trove, however. Leanne Mella, visual arts specialist at the United States Department of State, declared, "The John Margolies archive of photographs of American roadside architecture is acknowledged as the most comprehensive study of this subject extant." Soon, the State Department's Visual Arts Program that Mella directed mounted an exhibition of his work, *American Roadside Architecture*, that circulated for several years to embassies, consulates, and other institutions around the world, exposing global audiences to a seductive vision of America, every bit as powerful as Hollywood film. Citizens of the world could now see Margolies's images of flying-saucer-shaped gas stations, drive-ins, and moderne motels in such locations as Estonia, Ukraine, Hong Kong, and at the UNESCO headquarters in Paris. The landscape he had photographed, as it turned out, fascinated the rest of the world.

Margolies's unique archive of images is now becoming a public resource and a historical record. In his images, the strange sculpture gardens and oddball museums, the work of nearly forgotten geniuses live on. Now, the signs never fade, bearing their perfect, platonic ideals of hamburgers and whipped ice cream cones.

Like Herodotus verbally memorializing ancient civilizations, Margolies has spent his life visually recording a culture. He explored the carnival of roadside architecture to which 20th-century boom-time and automobile-mad America had given birth.

History will record that once upon a time a vast wealth of creativity spread across an almost empty land. And there a rich and unprecedented civilization rose. Beginning with the 1903 discovery of oil in Texas and accelerated by the introduction of the Model T Ford in 1908, this petroleum-fueled civilization laid ribbons of asphalt and concrete across a continent in just a few decades. By contrast with the more traditional landscapes of Europe or Asia, many of the roadside buildings along this American landscape were built in haste and were designed for speed reading, as opposed to the close-focus nature of traditional-world urban landscapes.

This architectural dialect represented a fundamental aspect of the American spirit. By documenting it in photographs and maintaining his collection, Margolies has, in essence, written a chapter of a national history, a chapter in the development of the American character. How else would we be able to explain to future generations that we went to drive-in restaurants where we once ate from car window trays brought to the car by waitresses on roller skates, ventured off the beaten path to sleep in concrete tepees, or explain to people of other nations that Americans once traveled in automobiles to sit in parking lots watching films projected onto giant white screens, producing flickering, soundless images visible from miles away?

The collected works of John Margolies provide visual proof of the genius and serendipity of the first era of American automobile culture.

VORWORT

C. Ford Peatross

Mehr als drei Jahrzehnte lang ist John Margolies kreuz und quer durch die USA gereist, ein leidenschaftlicher Entdecker mit einer klaren Mission. Mehr als 100 000 Meilen hat er auf der Suche nach außergewöhnlicher und landestypischer Straßenrandbebauung zurückgelegt. Mit seinen Tausenden von Fotografien und seiner einzigartigen Kollektion von Sammlerstücken wie Straßenkarten, Postkarten und Broschüren hat er die schwindenden Symbole einer mobilen Nation dokumentiert, die immerzu auf Achse ist und ihre eigene Geschichte dabei beständig ausradiert – auf diese Weise wurde sie für die Nachwelt gerettet.

John wurde mit Herodot, dem „Vater der Geschichtsschreibung", in Verbindung gebracht, der die antike Welt bereiste und beschrieb. Ich sehe in ihm eine Art Zirkusdirektor der „Architektur der Übertreibung", denn er weist uns auf die Einzigartigkeit und den Wert der gezeigten Objekte hin und präsentiert sie als wichtige Zeugnisse unserer nationalen, regionalen und persönlichen Identität. Diese aus einem unternehmerischen Geist geborenen Attraktionen, die oft riesengroße Dimensionen annehmen und eine überbordende Fantasie an den Tag legen, offenbaren die Originalität, den Einfallsreichtum, die Respektlosigkeit und die Chuzpe ihrer Schöpfer. Durch Johns Eifer und seinen vorausschauenden Blick haben wir diese Underdogs der Highways heute zu lieben und zum Teil sogar zu erhalten gelernt, auch wenn sie ständig vom Abriss bedroht sind.

Die Bilder in *Roadside America* offenbaren demonstrative Zurschaustellung, nicht Zurückhaltung. Wie das Licht Motten anzieht, sollen die Attraktionen Reisende anlocken und vom Weg abbringen wie einst die Sirenen mit ihrem Gesang. Diese Architektur ist oft anonym in ihrer Entstehung, sie ist kein autobiografischer Spiegel, sondern rein pragmatisch. Sie spricht unsere innersten Gefühle an, sei es durch ihre Platzierung, durch Form, Farbe und Beleuchtung, durch ihre Symbolhaftigkeit, Bewegung und mehr oder weniger explizite Botschaften. Hunger, Durst, Glauben, Eitelkeit, Sicherheit, Patriotismus, Komfort und Genuss sind nur einige der menschlichen Bedürfnisse, die sie in Konsumwünsche zu übersetzen versucht, damit Kunden auf ihre Parkplätze und durch die Eingänge hinein bis zur Kasse gelockt werden. Unterstützt durch neue Materialien und neue Technologien wie z. B. die freie Formbarkeit von bewehrtem Beton und das verführerische Blinken der Neonlichter ist die Freiheit des Ausdrucks in dieser Architektur beispiellos und ein einmaliges Produkt des amerikanischen Schmelztiegels, des Einfallsreichtums und freien Handels.

Es ist passend, dass diese große dokumentarische Sammlung nun zur besonderen Attraktion in einer der großartigsten Shows der Welt (und ihrer umfangreichsten Bibliothek) werden wird: in Amerikas ältester staatlicher Institution, der Library of Congress. Hier sind die Dokumente, Nachlässe und Werke aller Großen aus Architektur und Design zu finden.

Über dem Eingang zum Thomas Jefferson Building der Bibliothek steht eine Büste des berühmten Philosophen Ralph Waldo Emerson, in Stein gehauen von Jonathan Scott Hartley. Emerson vertrat die Überzeugung, dass Schönheit und Wahrheit nicht nur in den schönen Künsten zu finden seien, sondern auch im Gewöhnlichen, und dass die Beschäftigung mit „dem Nahen, dem Niedrigen, dem Gemeinen" entscheidend für die kreative Entwicklung einer jungen Nation sei. Tatsächlich gibt es nur Weniges, das wahrhaftiger uramerikanischer, demokratischer und individualistischer ist als die amerikanischen Ikonen, die John Margolies am Straßenrand entdeckt hat. Seine Bilder versprechen zu überdauern, zu inspirieren und zu informieren, noch lange nachdem die auf ihnen abgebildeten Artefakte verschwunden sind. Der große amerikanische Designer Charles Eames glaubte, gutes Design sei Ausdruck eines Zwecks und entspreche einem menschlichen Bedürfnis, auf das es reagiere. Demnach müsse es schon von seinem Wesen her vergänglich sein. „Es kann später (falls es gut genug ist) als Kunst beurteilt werden."

Und nun, um bei der Sprache der Zirkusarena zu bleiben: „Immer hereinspaziert, meine Damen und Herren, große und kleine Kinder ... wenn Sie Ihre geneigte Aufmerksamkeit nun auf die kommenden Seiten mit ihren wahnwitzigen, verblüffenden, schier unmöglich scheinenden, atemberaubenden Bildern richten würden – wir versprechen Ihnen Staunen, Wunder und Vergnügen!"

Phil Patton

John Margolies ist immer ganz früh unterwegs, damit der Himmel auf seinen Fotos schön blau aussieht. Früh morgens ist das Licht wunderschön, die ganze Welt wirkt sauber. „Ich liebe das Licht um diese Tageszeit, es ist wie goldgelber Sirup", sagt er. „Alles ist noch frisch und niemand stört einen beim Fotografieren."

An manche Morgen erinnert er sich besonders gut. Einmal fuhr er zum Beispiel zwei Stunden vor Sonnenaufgang los, um den Mother Goose Market in Hazard, Kentucky, zu fotografieren, ein ovales Gebäude mit eierförmigen Fenstern, auf dessen Dach eine fünf Meter hohe hölzerne Gans steht, deren Augen aus Autoscheinwerfern bestehen. Von solchen Anekdoten gibt es Hunderte. Wenn man sich mit Margolies unterhält, gewöhnt man sich daran, dass er ständig Ortsnamen anführt. Margolies gibt bereitwillig zu, dass er gewissermaßen in Anzeigetafeln denkt, und jedes seiner Bilder als autobiografisch empfindet.

„Trail Theater, Amarillo, Texas", deklamiert er dann, oder „Harold Warp's Pioneer Village, Minden, Nebraska", mit einer kräftigen Betonung jeden Namens. Oder: „Rockwood Motel, Klamath Falls, Oregon, Wigwam Motel, Holbrook, Arizona. Susie Q. Café, Mason City, Iowa."

John Margolies und wie er zu dem wurde, was er heute ist

John wuchs vor etlichen Jahrzehnten im wohlhabenden New Canaan, Connecticut, auf. Er verbrachte viele Stunden auf dem Rücksitz im Auto seiner Eltern auf Ausflügen, die häufig über den Berlin Turnpike bei Hartford führten, einen kurzen Straßenabschnitt, an dem es viele Geschäfte und Ampeln gab. Mit großen Augen betrachtete er die wunderbaren Läden am Straßenrand – Schnellrestaurants, Blockhütten, Autokinos und Billigtankstellen, die sich alle an diesem aufregenden Stück Highway drängten. Doch seine Eltern hielten nie an, außer vielleicht an einer der preiswerten Tankstellen; die Verlockungen der anderen Attraktionen ließen sie kalt.

Margolies ließ sich nicht beirren. Sobald er 16 war, machte er den Führerschein und war bald selbst in einem uralten 1948er Oldsmobile unterwegs, um all die Geschäfte am Straßenrand aufzusuchen, an denen seine Eltern so achtlos vorübergefahren waren: die Kinos und Kaufläden an den Hauptstraßen kleiner Städte, die Badeorte und Uferpromenaden, die Drive-in-Attraktionen und Touristenmekkas.

An der University of Pennsylvania, wo Margolies Journalismus und Kunstgeschichte studierte, begab er sich auf den Weg in die Welt der Architektur. 1962 machte er den Bachelor-Abschluss und wechselte dann für den Master an die Annenberg School of Communication. Dort belegte er einen Kurs bei Gilbert Seldes, damals einer der ganz wenigen Akademiker, die an amerikanischer Populärkultur interessiert waren, und Autor der Publikation *7 Lively Arts*, in der unter anderem Filme, Musicals und Comics eine Wertschätzung als Kunst erfuhren.

1964 schloss Margolies sein Studium mit einem Master of Arts in Kommunikationswissenschaften ab und arbeitete als Redaktionsassistent bei der renommierten Architektur- und Designzeitschrift *Architectural Record*. Später wurde er Programmleiter der Architectural League of New York, wo er 1970 für erste Kontroversen sorgte. Er zeigte eine Werkschau von Morris Lapidus, einem Architekten, der besonders für seine extravaganten Hotels im Hollywood-Stil bekannt war, zum Beispiel das Fontainebleau und das Eden Roc in Miami Beach – ein Affront gegen die konventionelle, moderne Ästhetik. Architekten wie Kritiker waren empört. Sie hielten Lapidus nicht für einen ernst zu nehmenden Architekten. „Die Leute waren entsetzt", erinnert sich Margolies. „Sie dachten, ich hätte den Verstand verloren."

Diesem Angriff auf den etablierten Geschmack folgte ein Artikel in *Progressive Architecture*, der ein Loblied auf das Madonna Inn in San Luis Obispo, Kalifornien, sang, dem berühmt-berüchtigten Flitterwochen-Palast, in dem jedes Zimmer nach einem anderen Thema dekoriert ist: Fels, Mammutbaum oder Grotte, das „Wolke-sieben-Zimmer", der Viktorianische Gartenraum, das Daisy-Mae- und das Höhlenmenschenzimmer.

Herkömmlicher Geschmack

Als Margolies in der Szene aufkreuzte, war die klassische Moderne noch all-beherrschend. Ornamente waren verpönt. Kleine Gasthäuser am Straßenrand waren mit der Entstehung des neuen Highway-Netzes verschwunden. Seit dem Federal-Aid Highway Act (1956) hatte die Regierung 25 Milliarden für den Autobahnbau bereitgestellt; alle „Super-Highways" wurden von nun an gleich gestaltet, ohne ebenerdige Kreuzungen und mit wenigen Auf- und Abfahrten.

Diese neuen Autobahnen schnitten viele alte Straßen vom Verkehr ab, wodurch die bunten, exzentrischen Geschäfte verkümmerten. Das Highway-Gesetz verbot den Bau von Raststätten und gewerblichen Unternehmen am Straßenrand. Durch diese Ausgangsbedingungen konnten sich die Restau-

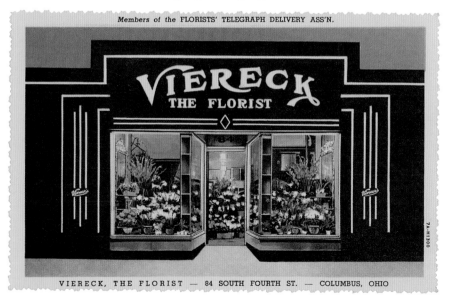

Members of the FLORISTS' TELEGRAPH DELIVERY ASS'N.

VIERECK, THE FLORIST — 84 SOUTH FOURTH ST. — COLUMBUS, OHIO

rantketten, die sich im ganzen Land an den Abfahrten ansiedelten, schnell ausbreiten. Nun, da die Autofahrer häufiger lange Strecken über Land fuhren, konnten sie sich überall an die immer gleichen Marken halten, die Sauberkeit und Zuverlässigkeit versprachen. Eigenwillige Lokale an den alten Straßen wirkten im Vergleich zu den als sicher und hygienisch wahr-genommenen Ketten nicht länger attraktiv.

Bei den neuen Autobahnen ging es ja nur noch ums Weiterkommen, um die schnellstmögliche Ankunft am Ziel. Dieses Konzept vom Reisen war für Margolies das Schlimmste, was er sich vorstellen konnte: Wieder wurde er daran gehindert anzuhalten und sich umzuschauen. Der Journalist Charles Kuralt brachte es mit seiner Aussage auf den Punkt, nun sei es erstmals mög-lich, die gesamten USA zu durchqueren, ohne irgendetwas zu sehen.

Margolies erinnert sich: „Ende der 1930er Jahre warnte der Leiter des FBI, J. Edgar Hoover, kleine Motels am Straßenrand seien der Nährboden für Laster und Gesetzlosigkeit." Die Präsidentengattin Lady Bird Johnson klagte über die Hässlichkeit der amerikanischen Straßen. In seinem einflussreichen Buch *God's Own Junkyard* verurteilte Architekt Peter Blake 1964 die Motels und American Diners.

Diese Ansichten setzten sich Mitte des Jahrhunderts auch bei den ameri-kanischen Automobilisten durch, ebenso wie bei einigen Unternehmern, die davon träumten, ihre kleinen Etablissements zu riesigen Ketten mit lauter gleichförmigen Ablegern auszuweiten. Das Unternehmen Shell Petroleum hatte schon früh den Weg zur Standardisierung aufgezeigt, indem es die Farbgebung und Beschilderung an all seinen Tankstellen vereinheitlichte.

Auch die Restaurantbesitzer wussten um die Wirkung eines vertrauten Erscheinungsbilds auf anspruchsvolle Autofahrer. Der Berühmteste von ihnen, Ray Kroc, erwarb die Rechte an der McDonald's-Hamburger-Kette, als er noch Vertreter für Milchshake-Mixer war, und baute einen vereinheitlichten Fran-chising-Giganten auf. Der Hotelier Kemmons Wilson gründete das Holiday Inn und vergab Konzessionen an Investoren in ganz Amerika, die neue Hotels nach den Design- und Dienstleistungsstandards des Unternehmens eröffneten.

Der Geist der Landstraße erwacht zu neuem Leben

Doch das Verhältnis der Amerikaner zur Straße und ihrer Bebauung war sehr viel solider und tiefer verwurzelt als der Modernismus oder das sterile kulturelle Klima der 1950er Jahre. Die USA pflegten ein langes Liebesverhältnis zum Automobil und seinem gesamten Umfeld. Die ersten „Motor Courts" gab es bereits in den 1920er Jahren und Minigolf war schon ab 1930 der letzte Schrei. Das erste Autokino öffnete 1933 in Camden, New Jersey, seine Pforten. Drive-in-Restaurants erfreuten sich seit den 1920er Jahren wachsender Beliebtheit.

Mit den Wirtschafts- und Sozialreformen des New Deal unter Franklin D. Roosevelt manifestierte sich die amerikanische Liaison mit der Straße und ihren Schrulligkeiten. Im Schriftstellerprogramm der Works Progress Administration entstand eine Reihe von Reiseführern und Geschichtsbüchern über die einzelnen amerikanischen Bundesstaaten. Wichtiger noch war das Fotografieprogramm der Farm Securities Administration, für das so bedeutende Fotografen wie Walker Evans, Dorothea Lange, Arthur Rothstein, John Vachon, Russell Lee, Marion Post Wolcott und Ben Shahn in allen Teilen des Landes unvergessliche Bilder aufnahmen. Diese Fotografen wussten die volkstümliche Bebauung des Straßenrands zu schätzen und machten zahlreiche Fotos von frühen Raststätten, so zum Beispiel von dem Imbiss in Hundeform, den Dorothea Lange 1939 in Oregon ablichtete.

Andere Fotografen der 1930er Jahre wie Edward Weston waren ebenfalls mit der Kamera auf Achse und schufen die Tradition der „Road Photography" – eine später von Robert Frank, Lee Friedlander, Stephen Shore und Jeff Brouws fortgeführte Tradition, die auch John Margolies aufgriff. Ohne es zu ahnen, suchte er Stätten auf, die Weston bereits dokumentiert hatte. „Es war der Super-Bowl-Sonntag 1979", erinnert sich Margolies. „Ich war im Mammy's Cupboard am Highway 61 nahe Natchez, Mississippi. Ich wusste nicht, dass Edward Weston das Restaurant 1940 ebenfalls fotografiert hatte."

Trotz des in den 1960er Jahren vorherrschenden Trends zu nüchternen Zweckbauten wurde das Werk dieser Architekturfotografen und mit ihnen der alte Geist der freien Landstraße wiederentdeckt. Die Kuratoren am Museum of Modern Art in New York präsentierten das Werk von Fotografen, die ihre Motive am zeitgenössischen Straßenrand fanden, wie Lee Friedlander und William Eggleston. 1968 – zwei Jahre bevor Margolies die Lapidus-Werkschau organisierte – zeigte das Newport Harbor Art Museum in Kalifornien unter dem Titel „Just Before the War" eine Auswahl der Arbeiten, die für die Farm Securities Administration entstanden waren.

Zudem wurde die Landstraße in Literatur und Film immer stärker glorifiziert: Sie symbolisierte ein amerikanisches Urerlebnis, das auf den Zug der Pioniere in den Wilden Westen, die Lewis-und-Clark-Expedition und Francis Parkmans Arbeiten zur Kolonialgeschichte zurückging.

Der Topos der Autofahrt quer durchs ganze Land entwickelte sich zum literarischen Genre; Duncan Hines und John Steinbeck zählten zu den bekanntesten amerikanischen Reiseschriftstellern. Das bekannteste Buch über das Leben auf der Straße war Jack Kerouacs *On the Road (Unterwegs)*. 1957, nur ein Jahr nach Einführung des Interstate Highway Programs veröffentlicht, erzählte es von der Kultur der Straße als Alternative zu den Freeways und Franchise-Ketten. Das Manuskript hatte die Form der Straße selbst – es bestand aus einer ca. 40 Meter langen Papierrolle. Während Kerouac seinen Roman schrieb, erhoben der Komponist John Cage und der Künstler Robert Rauschenberg eine Mini-Spritztour zum Kunstwerk: Sie fuhren mit dem tintenbeschmierten Reifen von Cages Ford Model A über eine Papierrolle.

Erste Vertreter des Roadmovie waren *Es geschah in einer Nacht* (1934) und *Im Schatten der Nacht* (1948). Seinen Höhepunkt fand das Genre in den späten 1960er und frühen 1970er Jahren mit Filmen wie *Bonnie und Clyde, Diebe wie wir* und *American Graffiti. Die letzte Vorstellung,* Peter Bogdanovichs Film über eine trostlose Kleinstadt irgendwo in Texas, bestand aus Schwarz-Weiß-Einstellungen, die an Fotos von Walker Evans erinnern.

Aus diesem Geist entstand auch Margolies' fotografisches Großvorhaben.

24

On the Road

Margolies nahm seine Fahrten kreuz und quer durchs Land Mitte der 1970er Jahre auf. In seinen Augen wurde die Kreativität und Individualität der alten, zweispurigen Landstraße, die er so liebte, von den grauen, vereinheitlichten Ketten der Interstate-Autobahnen vernichtet. Er beobachtete, wie diese Tradition immer weiter zurückging, und wurde sich bewusst, wie wichtig es war, sie zu dokumentieren, bevor sie ganz verschwunden war. Der Titel seines ersten Bildbandes wies bereits darauf hin: *The End of the Road: Vanishing Highway Architecture in America* („Das Ende der Straße: Amerikas verschwindende Highway-Architektur").

Sein Ziel war simple Dokumentation. „Ich habe praktisch keinerlei Ahnung von Fotografie", sagt er über sich selbst. Er blieb seinen altehrwürdigen Canon-Kameras über die Jahre hinweg treu und fotografierte fast ausschließlich mit 50-mm-Standardobjektiv und 25-ASA-Film – ein ‚langsamer' Film, wie Fotografen es nennen, mit dem sich eine maximale Farbsättigung erzielen lässt. Den Übergang zur Digitalfotografie hat er nicht mitgemacht.

Margolies verstand sich ebenso als Historiker wie als Fotograf; er erinnert sich an einen Nachmittag in Hamilton, New York, wo er 1978 eine Shell-Tankstelle fotografierte: „Ein Mann kam auf mich zu und wollte wissen: ‚Was machen Sie denn da? Wollen Sie das für die Nachwelt festhalten?' Wie sich herausstellte, wurden die Zapfsäulen am nächsten Morgen herausgerissen. Ich bewahrte sie also gewissermaßen wirklich für die Nachwelt."

Margolies unternahm seine Erkundungsreisen nach einem gleichbleibenden Muster: Los ging es im späten Frühling oder im Frühherbst, wenn keine Familien und Sommerurlauber die Straßen verstopften. Dann mietete er sich „das größte, bequemste und am besten gepolsterte amerikanische Auto", das sich finden ließ, und stellte im Radio einen Top-40-Sender ein. Er fuhr eine halbe Stunde nach dem ersten Morgengrauen los, nachdem er sämtliche Scheiben geputzt hatte, wie er es jeden Morgen tat, um die beste Sicht zu haben. Dann verschwanden die Hochhäuser Manhattans allmählich im Rückspiegel. Er fuhr, bis er hinaus aufs unverbaute Land kam. Sein Ziel war es, Städte, Ortschaften und Highways zu entdecken, die er noch nie zuvor gesehen hatte. Margolies beschreibt es so: „Mein größtes Ziel im Leben ist, überall hinzukommen und alles zu sehen." An der Erreichung dieses Ziels arbeitet er immer noch.

Er entwickelte ein System, das ihm ein Leben und Arbeiten in Autos und Motelzimmern erleichterte. Er führte nicht nur Kühltaschen mit sich, in denen die Filmrollen kühl gehalten wurden, sondern auch separate Taschen für Badezimmer und Verpflegung und andere Lebensnotwendigkeiten, die bei jedem Halt ganz systematisch ein- und ausgeladen wurden. Zu diesen Lebensnotwendigkeiten gehörten auch Landkarten, die er jeden Abend sorgfältig neu faltete, sodass die am nächsten Tag sich bietenden Möglichkeiten sichtbar waren, eine Reisetasse, ein faltbares Brett zur Versteifung von Matratzen mit Kartoffelbreikonsistenz, Wäscheklammern, damit die Vorhänge zublieben und niemand hereinschauen konnte, und ein Fred-Flintstone-Nachtlicht an einem 6-Meter-Verlängerungskabel, mit dem sich unbekannte Badezimmer ausleuchten ließen. Er hatte sogar eine Flitsche aus zwei verknoteten Gummibändern dabei, um gegen die Stubenfliegen anzugehen, die seine Unterkünfte regelmäßig mit ihm teilen zu wollen schienen.

War er erst einmal unterwegs, konnten ihn nur noch äußere Faktoren wie Wetter und Licht aufhalten. Einmal saß er wegen Regenwetters vier Nächte lang in einem Motel in Bedford, Pennsylvania, am Lincoln Highway fest und wartete darauf, dass es aufklarte. Er hatte sich in den Kopf gesetzt, ein spektakuläres Bauwerk zu verewigen: eine Taverne in Form einer Kaffeekanne. Als Himmel und Sonne ihm endlich gewogen waren, parkten leider einige Autos vor dem Gebäude. Da er aber darauf bestand, auf seinen Bildern keine Autos – „Zeitbezüge", wie er sie nennt, – auftauchen zu lassen, ging er in die Kneipe, erklärte sein Anliegen und bot allen Anwesenden an, ihnen einen Drink zu spendieren, wenn sie ihre Autos entfernten. Gesagt, getan, und Margolies bekam seine Aufnahme. Mission erfüllt.

John Margolies als Christoph Kolumbus

Aspekte des einen Ausflugs nahmen oft den Verlauf des nächsten vorweg. Auf der Fahrt durch den Mittleren Westen war er beeindruckt von einer Pocahontas-Statue, die im Örtchen Pocahontas, Iowa, aus einem Maisfeld ragte. Er war eigentlich auf dem Weg zum Corn Palace in Mitchell, South Dakota, einem Gebäude, das jedes Jahr zur Feier der reichen Ernte mit Maiskolben und -hülsen verziert wurde. In anderen Teilen South Dakotas fotografierte er Kleinstadtbanken, die mittlerweile als Kneipen genutzt wurden. In Rugby, North Dakota, schoss er ein Bild von einem Denkmal, das auf dem geografischen Mittelpunkt Nordamerikas steht. Unweit von Grassy Butte, North Dakota, begann Margolies' Wagen, unliebsame Geräusche von sich zu geben. Ein leider nicht sehr nahe gelegenes Ford-Autohaus diagnostizierte ein Problem mit dem Radlager und führte eine kostenlose Reparatur durch. In Great Falls, Montana, ließ Margolies seine Kamera fallen, während er einen stromlinienförmigen Busbahnhof fotografierte – eine potenzielle Katastrophe. Aber einmal schnell geschüttelt, einen Probefilm verschossen, und schon war klar, dass kein dauerhafter Schaden entstanden war. In Whitefish, Montana, fotografierte er einen zum Andenkenladen umfunktionierten Eisenbahnwaggon mit dem schönen Namen „The Caboose" und seinen Anbau „The Loose Caboose."

In der Nähe des Städtchens Opportunity überquerte er die Grenze von Idaho nach Washington. Er besuchte die Teapot Dome Service Station bei Zillah, ein Wunderwerk der 1920er Jahre in Form einer Teekanne. In Bend, Oregon, machte er eine wunderbare Entdeckung: Petersen's Rock Gardens, das Werk eines Exzentrikers namens Rasmus Petersen, der von 1935 bis 1952 einen Garten voll bizarrer Steinskulpturen angelegt hatte. In Klamath Falls nahm er das Rockwood Motel auf, das aus versteinertem Holz, Obsidian, Amethyst und anderen Mineralien gebaut war.

Und so erlebte er über dreißig Jahre lang auf über 100 000 Meilen endlose Abenteuer an den Straßen Amerikas. Es gab so viel mehr zu sehen, als er allein schaffen konnte. Irgendwann war er erschöpft von den Tausenden von Kilometern und endlosen Nächten unterwegs und wollte nur noch nach Hause.

Die Wohnung, in die er nach seinen Überlandfahrten zurückkehrte, war mit Schildern und anderen Andenken, die er von seinen Reisen mitbrachte, geschmückt, darunter auch Werbeschilder für längst vom Markt verschwundene Limonaden und Tankstellen. Historische Postkarten der von ihm aufgesuchten Gebäude standen in Drehständern auf dem Schreibtisch. Auch wenn die Postkarten ihm fast immer erst in die Hände fielen, wenn er das jeweilige Gebäude bereits fotografiert hatte, waren sie doch wichtig als Bezugspunkte, wie die Gebäude viele Jahre zuvor ausgesehen hatten, als sie neu waren. Sie bildeten einen Kontrast zu seinen eigenen, erst Jahrzehnte später entstandenen Bildern, die einen Zustand zeigten, der fast nie so gut war wie der auf den alten Postkarten.

Im Laufe der Jahrzehnte entstand aus den Postkarten, zusammen mit anderen Sammlerartikeln wie alten Straßenkarten, Fremdenverkehrsbroschüren und sogar Streichholzschachteln, eine wichtige Begleitsammlung zu Margolies' Fotoarchiv.

Margolies gewinnt an Fahrt

1916 schockierte Henry Ford die Menschen mit der Behauptung: „Geschichte ist Blödsinn!" Als Ford das sagte, wirkte er wie ein reaktionärer Trottel, aber in gewisser Weise war er ein Visionär. Er meinte damit, dass die Geschichte, so wie sie in den Geschichtsbüchern steht, einseitig und unvollständig ist. Er plädierte dafür, das zu studieren, was wir heute Alltagskultur nennen würden – die Objekte, die von normalen Menschen gemacht und benutzt werden. Ford sammelte zum Beispiel alte Gebäude: Wohnhäuser, Scheunen und Ladengeschäfte, die er im Greenfield Village in Dearborn, Michigan, ausstellte, weil er Geschichte so bewahren wollte, wie sie von den Menschen mit eigener Hand gemacht worden war. Er sagte: „Wenn man weiß, wie es geht, kann man einen Gegenstand so gut lesen wie ein Buch."

26

Ortschaften zu lesen wie Gegenstände, war genau das, was Margolies aus dem Effeff beherrschte. Die annähernd 200 Filme, die er pro Ausflug verschoss, wurden bei den Tausenden von Dias eingereiht, die er wie Bücher auf Regalen einer riesigen Bibliothek in seiner Wohnung und an zwei anderen sicheren Orten außerhalb der Stadt archivierte. Margolies' Bestandsaufnahme der amerikanischen Alltagskultur erhellte die Ära der aussterbenden Attraktionen am Straßenrand viel besser, als Worte allein es je vermocht hätten.

Fords Überzeugung fand ein Echo bei Margolies' Fürsprecher Philip Johnson. „Man kann die Geschichte nicht ignorieren", ist ein berühmter Ausspruch Johnsons. Er nahm damit Bezug auf die Abkehr der Postmoderne von der Ästhetik des ornamentlosen Betonkastens hin zum Verspielten, Kommerziellen. Johnson lobte Margolies für seine Dokumentation eines „vergessenen Teils des großen amerikanischen Architekturerbes" und nannte ihn „den vielleicht führenden Historiker auf diesem Gebiet". Der Architekturkritiker Paul Goldberger nannte ihn den „Vater einer ganzen Bewegung".

Anerkennung und Aufmerksamkeit für Margolies wuchsen und es wurde immer deutlicher, dass der von seiner Ausstellung für die Architectural League 1970 verursachte Skandal nur einen Streitpunkt innerhalb einer großen Übergangszeit dargestellt hatte. Der Modernismus verlor an mehreren Fronten an Boden. In den 1970er Jahren gab es die Ölkrise, die eine direkte Infragestellung der neuen Super-Highways mit ihrer Geschwindigkeitsideologie nach sich zog. Die amerikanischen Autofahrer wurden gezwungen, langsamer zu fahren und wieder an den ursprünglichen Geist der Landstraße anzuknüpfen.

1972 veröffentlichten Robert Venturi und Denise Scott Brown das bahnbrechende Werk *Learning from Las Vegas*, in dem sie sich für die Strip Mall, die Einkaufsmeile neben der Straße stark machten – besonders prominent natürlich als Strip in Las Vegas, aber auch am Stadtrand jeder amerikanischen Stadt und Ortschaft zu finden –, die auf die Frühzeit des Automobils zurückging. Sie waren fasziniert von der Populärarchitektur, die von den Modernisten so vehement abgelehnt wurde. Das Hauptaugenmerk der Autoren lag auf zwei Spielarten der „Architektur ohne Architekten": Zum einen gab es

den Typus der „verzierten Scheune", ein einfaches oder manchmal regelrecht primitives Gebäude, das mit zeichenhaften Botschaften oder durch ein großes, auffallendes und oft fantasievolles Zeichen an der Stirnseite Aufmerksamkeit auf sich zog, wie die Kasinos in Las Vegas mit ihrem spektakulären Neongeglitzer. Zum anderen gab es den Typus „Duck", ein Gebäude, dessen äußere Gestalt seine Bedeutung oder Funktion kommunizierte, etwa ein Café in Form einer Kaffeetasse oder -kanne.

Diese Kategorie des „mimetischen Gebäudes" hatte ihren Namen in Anlehnung an die „Big Duck" erhalten. Dabei handelt es sich um einen Geflügelmarkt in Long Island, der in einem riesigen entenförmigen Betongebäude untergebracht war, eine in der Region bekannte Sehenswürdigkeit, die zwar von Modernisten wie Peter Blake verhöhnt, aber von der Bevölkerung und von Venturi und Scott Brown geliebt wurde.

In *Learning from Las Vegas* stellten die Autoren die Behauptung auf, dass diese Art der Populärarchitektur mit ihrer Bildhaftigkeit und ihrem Symbolismus der „gehobenen Architektur" als Inspiration dienen könne. Margolies war da radikaler: „Venturi und Scott Brown waren der Ansicht, man könne von diesen Gebäuden lernen, um sich Inspiration für echte Architektur zu holen. Ich habe gesagt, das *ist* die echte Architektur."

Durch diese Auffassung wurde Margolies nicht nur Teil einer Gruppe postmoderner Architekten und Kritiker, sondern auch einer langsam, aber sicher an Einfluss gewinnenden Bewegung für den Denkmalschutz. 1977 wurde eine Organisation gegründet, die für die Wertschätzung und Dokumentation der Straßenraumgestaltung eintrat und sich „Society for Commercial Archaeology" nannte. Bald wurde die Aufnahme von Tankstellen und American Diners in das National Register of Historic Places, dem amerikanischen Verzeichnis aller für den Erhalt vorgeschlagenen Gebäude, beantragt. Zu dieser Zeit, als die amerikanische Populärmusik und die Populärkunst ein Revival erlebten, wurde auch die Populärarchitektur neu bewertet.

Anthropologen, Populärkulturwissenschaftler und Architekten schenkten der Straßenarchitektur nun ebenfalls größere Aufmerksamkeit. 1979 veröf-

fentlichten zwei Kollegen von Venturi und Scott Brown, Paul Hirschorn und Steven Izenour, ein Buch mit dem Titel *White Towers*, das sich mit der vereinheitlichten Architektur einer Hamburger-Kette beschäftigte. Im selben Jahr brachte Richard J. S. Gutman das Standardwerk *American Diner* heraus, das erste Buch über die Geschichte dieser Restaurantarchitektur, und Warren Belasco veröffentlichte *Americans on the Road: From Autocamp to Motel*, eine Untersuchung über Autoreisen in den USA von 1910 bis 1945. Ein Jahr später präsentierte Jim Heimann in seiner Publikation *California Crazy* eine bunte Palette „mimetischer Gebäude". John Baeders kombinierte in seinem Buch *Gas, Food and Lodging* (1982) Postkarten mit fotorealistischen Ölgemälden amerikanischer Diners. 1985 brachte Chester Liebs einen umfassenden Überblick über die Populärarchitektur am amerikanischen Straßenrand des 20. Jahrhunderts heraus: *Main Street to Miracle Mile*.

Währenddessen rückte Margolies langsam ins Zentrum des Interesses. Das Guggenheim Fellowship für Architekturkritik 1978 war eine der ersten wichtigen Finanzquellen für seine Arbeit, es folgten zahlreiche Stipendien des National Endowment for the Arts und 2003 ein großes Stipendium für Fotojournalismus von der Alicia Patterson Foundation. Diese und andere Fördergelder aus privaten und staatlichen Quellen ermöglichten ihm die Weiterführung seiner großen Rundfahrten. Er schätzt, dass er 1979 und 1980 eine von drei Nächten in einem Motel verbrachte.

1980 veranstaltete Margolies eine große Ausstellung im Cooper-Hewitt Museum of Design in New York City über Hotels in den Catskill Mountains, einer Ausflugsregion im Staat New York. Im folgenden Jahr würdigte Kurator Richard Koshalek vom Hudson River Museum in Yonkers, New York, seine Arbeit in einer Ausstellung mit dem Titel „The End of the Road". Die Bilder aus „The End of the Road" zeigen unterschiedliche Relikte der Straßenrandbebauung. Ein aufwendig gestaltetes Neonzeichen an einem Café zeigte eine idealisierte Kellnerin mit einem makellosen Milkshake vor einem grünen Tannenwald. Außerdem gab es viele Aufnahmen der Rückseiten von Autokino-Leinwänden, die manchmal mit verblassten, freskenhaften Wandmalereien

verziert waren. Die Fotos wirken nostalgisch – gegen Ende der 1970er Jahre begannen diese Gebäude und Attraktionen am Straßenrand zu verfallen.

Margolies' Bilder schafften im Laufe des Jahrzehnts den Sprung von den Museumswänden in diverse Bildbände. 1987 suchte er seine Aufnahmen von Minigolfplätzen für eine Geschichte dieses Sports von Nina Garfinkel und Maria Reidelbach zusammen. Der Umschlag bestand aus demselben Kunstrasen, der auch auf den Minigolfplätzen zu finden ist. Für die Publikation *Hitting the Road: The Art of the American Road Map* tat Margolies sich mit einem anderen Landkartensammler, Douglas A. Yorke Jr., und dem Designer Eric Baker zusammen. Unter dem Titel *Ticket to Paradise* gab Margolies, unterstützt von Emily Gwathmey, seine Fotos von Lichtspieltheatern in kleinen und größeren amerikanischen Städten heraus – Bijous und Odeons an oft heruntergekommenen Hauptstraßen. Mit diesen Büchern schuf und förderte Margolies das allgemeine Bewusstsein für das Kleinstadt-Amerika.

Vermächtnis

Margolies' Werk, das ihn auf der ganzen Welt berühmt werden ließ, erweckt eine Ära in der amerikanischen Geschichte zum Leben, die ansonsten in Vergessenheit geraten würde. Seine Bilder haben vielleicht gerade durch das ironisch wirkende Fehlen einer unmittelbaren emotionalen Ansprache eine starke Wirkung auf ihr Publikum. Ihre Geradlinigkeit und Abwesenheit visueller Schnörkel steigert ihre Aussagekraft im Laufe der Zeit noch. Die Bilder zeigen den Verfall und die Abnutzung, ohne sie romantisch zu verklären. Mit dem Verschwinden der ursprünglichen Motive hat sich deren Präsenz in den Bildern magisch verstärkt. In seinem Werk sind zahlreiche Artefakte zu sehen, die es nicht mehr gibt. Seine Fotografien haben im Laufe der Zeit ihre eigene Realität gewonnen, eine mythische Landschaft, in der manche von uns tatsächlich gelebt und von der wir alle schon geträumt haben.

Dank der Aussagekraft seiner Arbeit fand Margolies nicht nur in Amerika Anerkennung, sondern auch in Ecken der Welt, die von seiner Heimat weit

entfernt sind. 2004 wurde er von der Photographers Association of Macau geehrt. Als er 2009 eine Ausstellung in Rom hatte, wurde er vom italienischen Fernsehen interviewt, als sei er ein Modezar.

Margolies hat sein Amerika vorgeführt und die Besucher aufgeklärt und zum Teil auch dazu ermutigt, sich für den Schutz der Bauwerke einzusetzen. Er bewies einen verblüffenden Instinkt, direkt vor der Abrissbirne einzutreffen, was die Einwohner nach der Veröffentlichung seiner Bilder dazu ermutigte, selbst als Denkmalschützer aktiv zu werden.

Der Wert von Margolies' Fotoarchiv und Sammlung als unbezahlbarer Ressource ist nach und nach in das öffentliche Bewusstsein gedrungen. C. Ford Peatross, Leiter des Center for Architecture, Design and Engineering in der Abteilung Druck und Fotografie an der Library of Congress erkannte die Bedeutung der Fotografien und setzte Bemühungen in Gang, sie für die Library of Congress – und damit für das amerikanische Volk – zu erwerben.

Peatross war nicht der Einzige, der den Wert dieses Schatzes erkannte. Leanne Mella, Spezialistin für bildende Künste im amerikanischen Außenministerium, erklärte: „Das John Margolies Archiv mit seinen Fotografien amerikanischer Straßenraumgestaltung ist anerkanntermaßen die umfassendste Studie, die zu diesem Thema existiert." Bald danach veranstaltete das Visual Arts Program des State Department, dessen Direktor Mella war, unter dem Titel „American Roadside Architecture" eine Werkausstellung, die mehrere Jahre lang um die ganze Welt wanderte. Einem weltweiten Publikum wurde auf diese Weise ein verführerisches Bild Amerikas vor Augen geführt, was nicht weniger wirksam war als ein Hollywoodfilm. Menschen in Estland, der Ukraine, Hongkong oder im UNESCO-Hauptquartier in Paris sahen Margolies' Bilder von Tankstellen in Form von fliegenden Untertassen, Drive-ins und modernen Motels. Wie sich herausstellte, war auch der Rest der Welt fasziniert von den Landschaften, die er fotografierte.

Margolies' einzigartiges Archiv ist eine heute öffentlich zugängliche historische Sammlung. In seinen Bildern leben die seltsamen Skulpturengärten und kuriosen Museen mit ihren Werken vergessener Genies weiter. Diese Ne-

onzeichen werden nie verlöschen und immer ihre Idealbilder von Hamburgern und Softeiswaffeln zeigen.

Ähnlich wie Herodot, der antike Zivilisationen mit seinen Worten unsterblich machte, verbrachte Margolies sein Leben damit, eine Kultur in Bildern aufzuzeichnen. Er hat den Jahrmarkt der Straßenarchitektur erforscht, der im autoverrückten Amerika des zwanzigsten Jahrhunderts aus dem Wirtschaftsboom entstanden ist.

In den Geschichtsbüchern wird stehen, dass es einst einen riesigen Reichtum an Kreativität gab, der über ein fast leeres Land verteilt war. Dort entstand eine hochentwickelte, neue Art von Zivilisation. Angefangen mit den ersten Erdölfunden 1903 in Texas, beschleunigt durch die Einführung des Ford Model T 1908, durchzog diese benzingetriebene Zivilisation innerhalb weniger Jahrzehnte einen ganzen Kontinent mit Bändern aus Asphalt und Beton. Im Gegensatz zur traditionelleren Bauweise in Europa oder Asien wurden viele der Gebäude am Straßenrand hastig errichtet, für den schnellen Blick im Vorbeifahren, anders als die Stadtlandschaften der alten Welt, die langsam und eingehend betrachtet werden wollen.

Diese architektonische Spielart stellt einen wesentlichen Teil des *American Spirit* dar. Durch die Bilddokumentation und Pflege seiner Sammlung hat Margolies ein Kapitel der amerikanischen Geschichte geschrieben, ein Kapitel über die Entwicklung des amerikanischen Volkscharakters. Wie sollten wir zukünftigen Generationen ohne seine Bilder erklären können, dass wir früher in Drive-in-Restaurants fuhren, in denen man von Tabletts aß, die von Kellnerinnen auf Rollschuhen ans Autofenster gebracht wurden? Dass wir in Indianerzelten aus Beton schliefen, wenn wir etwas Besonderes unternehmen wollten? Wie sollten wir Menschen aus anderen Ländern deutlich machen, dass Amerikaner früher auf große Parkplätze fuhren, wo sie im Auto saßen und sich Filme anschauten, die auf riesige weiße Wände projiziert wurden, flackernde, lautlose Bilder, die auch noch in meilenweiter Entfernung zu sehen waren?

Mit seinem Werk verewigt John Margolies den Geist und das Glück der ersten Ära amerikanischer Automobilkultur.

30

AVANT-PROPOS

C. Ford Peatross

Pendant plus de trente ans, John Margolies, explorateur investi d'une mission, a sillonné les États-Unis avec une ferveur infaillible. Au cours de sa carrière, il a parcouru plus de 160 000 km pour débusquer des exemples d'architectures uniques et typiques au bord des routes secondaires et des rues principales d'innombrables petites villes américaines de province. Ses milliers de photographies originales et sa riche collection de documents imprimés d'époque – cartes routières, cartes postales, prospectus, etc. – rendent compte, en les préservant, des symboles éphémères d'une nation elle-même toujours sur la route et, en route, effaçant perpétuellement sa propre histoire.

John a été comparé à Hérodote, qui avait aussi en son temps parcouru son monde afin que la postérité en garde trace. Je le vois comme le Monsieur Loyal de ce qu'on pourrait appeler « l'architecture de l'hyperbole » ; il nous tranquillise, en affirmant que les objets qu'il a choisis sont remarquables, respectables, et qu'ils sont des manifestations de notre identité nationale, locale et personnelle. Audacieuses, souvent de dimensions exagérées, fruits d'une imagination fantastique, ces attractions de bord de route expriment l'originalité, les lubies, l'irrévérence et le culot de leurs créateurs. Grâce à l'assiduité et à l'œil précurseur de John, nous avons pu apprécier, célébrer et parfois préserver ces victimes de nos autoroutes et de nos déviations, alors même qu'elles sont menacées de démolition et qu'on réfléchit à ce qui les remplacera.

Les images de *Roadside America* dépeignent l'ostentatoire, pas le discret. Leurs sujets ont été conçus pour détourner le voyageur de son chemin, comme la flamme captive le papillon de nuit, ou la sirène, le marin. Leurs créateurs restent le plus souvent anonymes. Leur intention n'est pas autobiographique, mais purement pragmatique. Elles parlent à l'essence même de nos sensibilités, de par leur situation, leur forme, leurs couleurs, leur éclairage, leur symbolisme, leur mouvement, leur graphisme ou les autres messages qu'elles dispensent. La faim, la soif, la vanité, la sécurité, le patriotisme, la foi, le confort et le plaisir ne sont que quelques-uns des besoins humains élémentaires qu'elles tentent de transposer en désir commercial, pour attirer les clients sur leurs parkings, leur faire franchir la porte et passer à la caisse. Attisée par les nouveaux matériaux et les nouvelles technologies, comme les qualités plastiques du béton armé et l'éclairage aguicheur diffusé par les tubes néon, la liberté d'expression qui transpire de ces créations architecturales est sans précédent ; elle est aussi un pur produit du *melting pot*, de l'ingéniosité et du sens du commerce américains.

Il est logique que cette précieuse collection documentaire devienne un des pôles d'attraction d'un des plus célèbres lieux d'exposition du monde (et de sa plus vaste bibliothèque), la Bibliothèque du Congrès, la plus ancienne institution culturelle américaine. Elle renferme notamment les documents, archives et travaux des plus grands noms de l'architecture et du design.

L'entrée du bâtiment Thomas Jefferson de la bibliothèque est surplombée d'un buste du génie visionnaire Ralph Waldo Emerson, réalisé par Jonathan Scott Hartley. Emerson soutenait que la vérité et la beauté ne se trouvaient pas seulement dans les beaux-arts, mais aussi dans la vie ordinaire, et qu'il était crucial d'explorer « le proche, le bas, le commun » pour le développement créatif d'une jeune nation. De fait, il existe peu de choses plus profondément américaines, démocratiques et individualistes que les icônes des bords de route et des rues principales immortalisées par John Margolies. Ces images perdureront, inspireront et informeront le public longtemps après la disparition des lieux qu'elles représentent. Le grand designer américain Charles Eames pensait qu'un bon design est l'expression pragmatique et la réponse apportée à un besoin, et qu'il est donc forcément éphémère. « Il pourra ensuite (s'il est suffisamment bon) être considéré comme de l'art. »

Maintenant, à la manière d'un Monsieur Loyal, je vous fais l'annonce suivante : « Mesdames et messieurs, enfants petits et grands… Veuillez concentrer votre attention sur les pages qui suivent, sur ces images stupéfiantes, époustouflantes, ces réalisations de haut vol qui défient souvent toutes les lois physiques et esthétiques ! Vous en sortirez émerveillé, informé et ravi ! »

INTRODUCTION

Phil Patton

John Margolies se lève toujours de bonne heure pour saisir ses ciels bleus. Peu de gens sont debout, la lumière est magnifique et le monde semble plus propre. « J'adore la lumière à cette heure de la journée, on dirait du sirop doré », dit-il. « Tout est frais et personne ne vient me déranger. »

Certains de ces matins sont encore gravés dans sa mémoire. Comme celui où il prit la route deux heures avant l'aube pour arriver au bon moment à Hazard (Kentucky) et prendre en photo le Mother Goose Market, un bâtiment circulaire en pierre aux fenêtres en forme d'œuf, surmonté d'une oie en bois de plus de 4,60 m de haut dont les yeux étaient des phares de voiture. Un moment unique parmi des milliers d'autres. Lorsqu'on discute assez longtemps avec Margolies, on s'habitue à l'entendre ponctuer ses phrases de noms de lieux, comme s'il souhaitait ajouter des légendes à ses propos. Margolies est le premier à admettre sa « mentalité de collectionneur », et il considère chacun de ses clichés comme un témoignage autobiographique.

C'est ainsi qu'il déclame des appellations topographiques comme « Trail Theater, Amarillo, Texas » ou « Village pionnier de Harold Warp, Minden, Nebraska » en articulant chaque mot avec une lente emphase.

« Rockwood Motel, Klamath Falls, Oregon. »

« Wigwam Motel, Holbrook, Arizona. »

« Susie Q. Café, Mason City, Iowa. »

Les jeunes années de John Margolies

Il y a quelques dizaines d'années, il vécut une enfance paisible à New Canaan, (Connecticut). Il passa des heures sur la banquette arrière de la voiture familiale lors de balades qui les conduisaient parfois à l'est de Hartford, sur la Berlin Turnpike, une portion d'autoroute de quelques kilomètres interrompue par de nombreux feux de signalisation. Il observait avec émerveillement les enseignes hautes en couleur qui la bordaient : *diners* (petits restaurants), bungalows pour touristes, cinémas en plein air, stations-service concurrentes. Il se souvient pourtant que ses parents ne s'arrêtaient jamais dans ces établissements, sauf peut-être pour un plein d'essence pas trop cher. Les autres antres de bas-côtés les laissaient apparemment indifférents.

Margolies avait déjà une idée précise de la route qui serait la sienne, et rien ne l'en détournerait. Dès qu'il eut 16 ans, il obtint son permis de conduire. Presque aussitôt, à bord d'une Oldsmobile de 1948 plus que défraîchie, il retourna vers les attractions de bord d'autoroute qu'il voyait défiler trop vite quelques années plus tôt : sur les rues principales des petites villes, les cinémas et les épiceries, les promenades et résidences hôtelières le long des plages, les parcs d'attraction et les mecques touristiques de tous acabits.

Une fois à l'Université de Pennsylvanie, où il étudia le journalisme et l'histoire de l'art, il se passionna pour l'architecture. Diplômé en 1962, il décida de poursuivre son cursus à l'Annenberg School of Communication, où il assista aux cours du célèbre critique d'art Gilbert Seldes, grand spécialiste et défenseur de la culture populaire américaine, notamment de la comédie musicale et de la bande dessinée, dont il fit l'éloge dans son livre *7 Lively Arts*.

Margolies décrocha sa maîtrise de communication en 1964 et devint rédacteur en chef adjoint de la revue *Architectural Record*. Mais c'est en tant que directeur de la programmation de l'Architectural League de New York qu'il déclencha pour la première fois la controverse. En 1970, il y monta une exposition consacrée au travail de Morris Lapidus, connu pour ses extravagants hôtels hollywoodiens, comme le Fontainebleau et l'Eden Roc de Miami Beach, qui faisaient voler en éclats l'esthétique moderniste conventionnelle, dont les apôtres n'éprouvaient que mépris pour Lapidus. « Les gens étaient horrifiés », se souvient Margolies. « Ils ont cru que j'avais perdu la tête. »

Ce coup de boutoir contre la tendance dominante fut suivi d'un article de la revue *Progressive Architecture* qui saluait la réussite du Madonna Inn de San Luis Obispo, en Californie, archétype du palace pour lunes de miel, aux chambres thématiques : Pierre, Cèdre, Grotte, Septième ciel, Jardin anglais, Daisy Mae, Homme des cavernes...

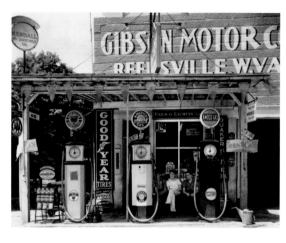

PREVIOUS SPREAD Everglades Safari Billboard, Dade County, Florida, 1980

LEFT Walker Evans, Filling Station, Reedsville, West Virginia, 1935

OPPOSITE Texaco Gas Station, Marietta, Ohio, 1976

Le goût du plus grand nombre

À l'époque où Margolies fit irruption dans le monde de l'architecture, le modernisme tenait toujours le haut du pavé. L'ornement était considéré avec dédain, et l'architecture hétéroclite des commerces indépendants de bord de route souffrait d'un mépris plus grand encore, surtout depuis l'avènement du système autoroutier moderne et de la nouvelle architecture qui l'accompagna. En 1956, le Federal-Aid Highway Act avait alloué vingt-cinq milliards de dollars à l'extension du réseau, en vertu de chartes techniques et esthétiques précises, qui excluaient notamment les bretelles et les intersections.

Ces tentacules de bitume contournaient les anciennes voies de circulation, condamnant à la décrépitude une multitude de petits commerces pittoresques. Le Highway Act interdit aussi la construction de stations-service ou d'établissements commerciaux en bordure de ces nouvelles artères rapides. Ces contraintes favorisèrent la croissance des chaînes commerciales. Les Américains se déplaçaient plus vite, allaient plus loin et appréciaient de pouvoir retrouver leurs produits, leurs marques, la présentation propre et rassurante des enseignes nationales. Ils se détournèrent des gargotes et petites boutiques biscornues au profit des allées immaculées des hypermarchés.

Le but des exploitants des autoroutes inter-États était de les faire rouler, de les acheminer le plus rapidement possible d'un endroit à un autre. Pour Margolies, cette approche du voyage était la pire qu'on puisse imaginer : c'était une autre façon d'empêcher les gens de s'arrêter pour regarder. Comme le souligna alors le journaliste et reporter Charles Kuralt, il était désormais possible de traverser le pays sans jamais rien « voir ».

Margolies se souvient : « À la fin des années 1930, J. Edgar Hoover, qui était alors à la tête du FBI, a averti la population contre les dangers des motels de bord de route, des coupe-gorge ou des bordels pour la plupart, lieux de vice et d'illégalité. » De son côté, la Première Dame, Lady Bird Johnson, déplora la laideur des bas-côtés américains. Dans son célèbre livre de 1964, *God's Own Junkyard*, l'architecte Peter Blake mit au pilori *motels* et *diners*.

Cette vision des choses donna des idées aux automobilistes des années 1950, et à certains entrepreneurs qui virent l'avantage qu'ils auraient à transformer leurs petits commerces locaux en vastes franchises aseptisées. La compagnie Shell jeta les bases de l'uniformisation commerciale en dotant toutes ses stations-service de la même signalétique et des mêmes couleurs, émaillant les routes de leur logo lumineux en coquille Saint-Jacques.

De la même manière, les propriétaires de restaurants comprirent le besoin de repères des automobilistes et se franchisèrent pour leur fournir un menu et des produits familiers, rassurants. C'est ainsi que Ray Kroc racheta la franchise des hamburgers de McDonald alors qu'il était vendeur ambulant de mixeurs multifonctions, et donna naissance à une des entreprises les plus célèbres du monde. Dans le domaine hôtelier, Kemmons Wilson créa à cette époque la chaîne Holiday Inn, et fit pulluler ses motels standardisés, identiques jusque dans les moindres détails.

Raviver l'esprit de la Route

Les racines de la relation que l'Amérique entretient avec la route et son architecture sont plus profondes qu'on l'imagine, et dans un sol plus fertile que celui dont se nourrirent le conformisme moderniste et le climat aseptisé des années 1950. L'Amérique était amoureuse de l'automobile, elle aima l'architecture créée pour la voiture, et ce, depuis le tout début. Les premiers *motels* apparurent dans les années 1920, dix ans plus tard le golf miniature devint une obsession nationale, et le premier *drive-in* fut inauguré à Camden, dans le New Jersey, en 1933. Les restaurants *drive-in* se multiplièrent aussi à partir des années 1920.

Grâce au New Deal de Franklin D. Roosevelt, l'Amérique dispose d'un riche témoignage de ce lien entre l'Amérique et ses excentricités routières. Les rédacteurs de la Works Progress Administration ont en effet publié une collection complète de livres historiques et de guides. Plus important encore, le service photographique de la Farm Securities Administration envoya dans tout le pays plusieurs photographes célèbres, parmi lesquels Walker Evans, Dorothea Lange, Arthur Rothstein, John Vachon, Russell Lee, Marion Post Wolcott ou Ben Shahn. Ces photographes avaient aussi une tendresse particulière pour les établissements de bas-côtés, notamment pour les vieux restaurants routiers, comme ce *diner* en forme de chien qu'immortalisa Dorothea Lange en 1939, dans l'Oregon.

D'autres photographes des années 1930, comme Edward Weston par exemple, interrompirent leurs voyages en voiture pour saisir les créations fantaisistes de leurs concitoyens. Ensemble, ils créèrent la tradition du photographe itinérant – une tradition ensuite perpétuée par Robert Frank, Lee Friedlander, Stephen Shore et Jeff Brouws, dont Margolies est un des derniers héritiers. Sans le savoir, il revisita certains des endroits qui avaient attiré l'objectif de Weston, un de ses prédécesseurs les plus brillants. « C'était le dimanche du Super Bowl, en 1979 », se souvient-il. « J'étais au Mammy's Cupboard, sur la Highway 61, pas loin de Natchez, dans le Mississippi. Et j'ignorais à ce moment-là qu'Edward Weston avait photographié ce même restaurant en 1940. »

Malgré la prédominance du goût moderniste, les années 1960 connurent aussi un retour en grâce de l'œuvre de ces photographes, ainsi que du vieil esprit de la route. Les conservateurs du musée d'Art moderne de New York mirent à l'honneur leurs héritiers, notamment Lee Friedlander et William Eggleston. En 1968 – deux ans avant que Margolies monte l'exposition Lapidus show –, le musée californien de Newport Harbor présenta une sélection des clichés pris par les employés de la FSA, sous le titre « Juste avant la guerre ».

L'horizon infini offert par la route prit aussi des allures héroïques dans la littérature et au cinéma. Prendre la route fait partie des expériences constitutives de l'esprit américain, forgé par la ruée vers l'Ouest racontée en détail par Lewis et Clark, ou l'histoire de Francis Parkman.

Raconter un trajet en voiture devient un genre littéraire en soi, embrassé par certains des auteurs américains les plus illustres, entre autres Duncan Hines et John Steinbeck. Le roman emblématique de ce mouvement demeure *Sur la route* de Jack Kerouac. Publié en 1957, un an seulement après le lan-

cement de l'Interstate Highway Program, il fit redécouvrir une autre manière de voyager, en marge des autoroutes géantes et des franchises. Le manuscrit était lui-même un chemin, puisqu'il se présentait sous la forme d'un rouleau de papier de quelque 36 m de long. Environ à l'époque où Kerouac noircissait ces mètres de papier, le compositeur John Cage et l'artiste Robert Rauschenberg réalisèrent un mini *road-trip* artistique en faisant rouler la Ford A de Cage sur un ruban de papier, après avoir enduit les pneus d'encre.

Le genre du *road-trip* s'illustre au cinéma dès 1934, avec *It Happened One Night*, puis avec *Les Amants de la nuit* en 1948. Il s'épanouit à la fin des années

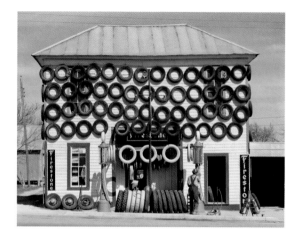

LEFT Don's Trading Post, Christiansburg, Virginia, 1982

FAR LEFT Russell Lee, Second-hand Tires Displayed for Sale, San Marcos, Texas, 1940

OPPOSITE Russell Lee, Hatchery Sign, Petaluma, California, 1942

1960 et au début des années 1970 avec des films mythiques comme *Bonnie and Clyde, Nous sommes tous des voleurs* ou *American Graffiti. La dernière séance*, le film de Peter Bogdanovich sur une petite ville du Texas rural, fut tourné en noir et blanc dans un style qui rappelle les photos de Walker Evans.

C'est dans cette atmosphère, et dans cet esprit, que naquit l'aventure photographique personnelle de Margolies.

Sur la route

Margolies prit la route au milieu des années 1970. Pour lui, la culture fade et standardisée du commerce franchisé que l'autoroute avait apportée avec elle était en train de tuer la créativité et l'individualité des bords de routes à deux voies qu'il chérissait tant. Il la voyait déjà disparaître et comprit qu'il était essentiel d'enregistrer sa présence avant qu'il soit trop tard. Le titre de son premier recueil de photos témoigne de cette ligne directrice : « La fin de la route – L'architecture routière américaine en voie de disparition ».

Son objectif n'était pas seulement documentaire, même s'il assure ne « presque pas » s'y connaître en photographie. Tout au long de sa carrière, il resta fidèle à la vénérable marque Canon. Il débuta avec un boîtier 50 mm de base et des pellicules à 25 ASA, à exposition lente, qui permettaient de saturer les couleurs au maximum. Il n'abandonna jamais l'argentique au profit du numérique.

Margolies est presque autant historien que photographe. Il se souvient d'une après-midi de 1978, à Hamilton (État de New York), où il s'arrêta dans une station Shell. « Un homme est venu vers moi et m'a demandé : "Qu'est-ce que vous faites, vous fixez cet endroit pour la postérité ?" Il se trouve que les pompes que j'étais en train de photographier devaient être démontées le lendemain. Effectivement, je fixais cette station-service pour la postérité. »

Les voyages de Margolies suivent un motif récurrent. Il part à la fin du printemps ou début septembre, avant ou après le passage massif des familles et hordes de touristes sur les routes. Il raconte qu'il loue toujours « la plus grosse, la plus confortable et la plus rembourrée des voitures américaines »

qu'il peut trouver, et qu'il cale l'auto-radio sur le Top 40. Le jour du départ, il lave consciencieusement ses pare-brises, comme il le fait ensuite chaque matin, pour voir le paysage le plus clairement possible. Il prend le volant une demi-heure après l'aurore, s'éloignant tranquillement des gratte-ciel de Manhattan qu'il regarde disparaître dans son rétroviseur. Il roule jusqu'à ce que l'horizon s'ouvre sur la campagne. À partir de cet instant, son seul but est de découvrir des villages, des hameaux et des routes qu'il n'a encore jamais vus. Margolies le dit très bien lui-même : son « principal objectif dans la vie est d'aller partout et de tout voir ». Cet objectif, il le poursuit encore aujourd'hui.

Au fil des années, il a appris à vivre et à travailler entre voitures et chambres de motel. En plus des glacières qu'il utilise pour garder les pellicules au frais, il transporte deux sacs destinés à ses salles de bains et cuisines successives, ainsi que d'autres objets essentiels qu'il décharge et recharge méthodiquement à chaque étape. Parmi ces biens de première nécessité figurent des cartes (qu'il déplie avec précaution tous les soirs pour prévoir son trajet du lendemain), sa tasse de voyage, une planche de couchage repliable pour combattre l'effet « sac de patates » de certains matelas, des pinces à linge pour tendre les draps lui garantissant un semblant d'intimité et une lampe veilleuse Fred Flintstone munie d'une rallonge de six mètres pour éclairer les cabinets de toilette les moins engageants. Il voyage aussi avec une fronde formée de deux bandes de caoutchouc entrelacées qui constitue, d'après son expérience, l'arme la plus efficace contre les mouches avec lesquelles il est trop souvent obligé de cohabiter.

Une fois sur la route, Margolies ne s'intéresse plus qu'à la météo et à la lumière. Un jour, il regarda tomber la pluie pendant quatre longues journées à Bedford, en Pennsylvanie, le long de la Lincoln Highway, attendant le moment propice pour immortaliser une relique spectaculaire : une taverne en forme de cafetière géante. Lorsque le ciel et le soleil s'accordèrent enfin à sa vision de l'endroit, il se dirigea vers le restaurant et découvrit une poignée de voitures garées sur le parking. Or il tenait à prendre des photos sans voitures – de nuisibles « références temporelles », selon lui. Il entra donc dans l'établis-

sement, expliqua ce qu'il faisait et annonça qu'il offrirait un verre à ceux qui iraient déplacer leurs voitures. Tous les clients obtempérèrent et Margolies put prendre sa photo. Mission accomplie.

John Margolies en Christophe Colomb

Il arrive aussi que les fragments d'un voyage rappellent les bribes des autres. Un jour qu'il traversait le Midwest en direction du Corn Palace de Mitchell (Dakota du Sud) – un monument érigé en hommage à la céréale reine de l'agriculture intensive, décoré chaque année d'épis nouveaux – il fut stupéfait de voir dépasser des champs de maïs, au niveau de la ville de Pocahontas (Iowa), une haute statue de l'héroïne indienne. Dans d'autres recoins du Dakota du Sud, il photographia des petites banques locales transformées en bars. À Rugby (Dakota du Nord), il prit en photo un panneau de signalisation indiquant le centre géographique de l'Amérique du Nord. Près de Grassy Butte (Dakota du Nord), la voiture de Margolies se mit à émettre un son inquiétant ; le concessionnaire Ford relativement le plus proche diagnostiqua un problème de direction, qu'il répara gratuitement. À Great Falls (Montana), Margolies laissa tomber un de ses appareils – catastrophe potentielle –, alors qu'il photographiait un arrêt de bus joliment profilé ; il lui suffit de le secouer et de vérifier la lentille pour se rendre compte que les dégâts n'étaient pas graves. À Whitefish (Montana), il photographia un tramway reconverti en une boutique de cadeaux baptisée « The Caboose » (« le wagon de queue »), avec son annexe le « Loose Caboose » (le « wagon de queue branlant »).

Il traversa l'Idaho jusqu'à l'État de Washington en passant près de la ville d'Opportunity. Il alla voir la station-service « Teapot Dome », près de Zillah, un bâtiment des années 1920 en forme de théière. À Bend (Oregon), il fit une découverte étonnante : les jardins de pierre de Petersen, un amoncellement bizarre de roches sculptées créé par l'excentrique Rasmus Petersen entre 1935 et 1952. À Klamath Falls, il prit en photo le Rockwood Motel, constitué de bois pétrifié et de minéraux comme l'obsidienne et l'améthyste.

C'est ainsi que la vie itinérante et aventureuse choisie par Margolies lui fit parcourir quelque 160 000 km en une trentaine d'années. Il y a tant de choses à voir en Amérique ! Quand les kilomètres d'asphalte et les innombrables nuits sur la route finissent par avoir raison de son enthousiasme, il revient chez lui, épuisé.

L'appartement qu'il prend plaisir à retrouver au retour de chacun de ses voyages est décoré de panneaux de signalisation et d'autres souvenirs glanés au fil du temps, notamment d'anciennes plaques métalliques faisant la promotion de marques de sodas ou d'essence disparues. Un présentoir en tourniquet, garni de cartes postales montrant les établissements qu'il a photographiés, trône sur le bureau. Margolies a reçu la plupart de ces cartes commerciales après être passé sur les lieux, mais elles font penser à des images de repérage, qui auraient été prises des décennies plus tôt pour témoigner de l'allure originelle de ces endroits. Les photos de Margolies montrent ce qu'ils sont devenus et, le plus souvent, la décrépitude a fait son œuvre.

Au fil des décennies, les cartes postales et autres objets éphémères ramassés sur la route, comme de vieilles cartes routières, des brochures touristiques ou même des boîtes d'allumettes, ont formé une collection qui complète admirablement les archives photographiques de Margolies.

Margolies atteint des sommets

En 1916, Henry Ford choqua le public en déclarant : « L'Histoire, ce ne sont que des bêtises. » Le magnat de l'automobile apparut comme le dernier des rustres réactionnaires, mais en un sens il fut visionnaire. Ce qu'il voulait dire, c'était que l'Histoire racontée dans les livres était limitée, distordue. Il militait en revanche pour l'étude de ce que nous appelons aujourd'hui la culture matérielle – ces objets fabriqués et utilisés par des gens ordinaires. Ford collectionnait les bâtiments anciens : il rassembla ses maisons, granges et échoppes pour créer le village de Greenfield à Dearborn, dans le Michigan, espérant préserver ainsi l'histoire populaire telle que façonnée par le peuple

38

américain lui-même. « Un objet », affirmait-il, « peut se lire comme un livre, si l'on sait comment s'y prendre. »

S'il y avait une chose que Margolies savait faire, c'était bien de lire les villes comme on lit les objets. Les quelque 200 pellicules qu'il utilisait pendant chaque périple rejoignaient des milliers d'autres boîtes de diapositives entreposées sur des étagères, comme des livres justement, dans la vaste bibliothèque de son appartement et dans deux autres lieux sûrs, en dehors de la ville. L'étude de la culture matérielle américaine ainsi réalisée par Margolies décrit mieux l'agonie des attractions populaires de bord de route que les mots sauraient le faire.

Le sentiment exprimé par Ford fut repris par un contemporain de Margolies, Philip Johnson. Le célèbre architecte, qui passa la fin de sa vie à New Canaan, eut cette phrase : « On ne peut pas ne pas connaître l'Histoire. » Il se réjouit de l'entrée en scène du postmodernisme, qui s'éloignait de l'esthétique épurée, froide et bétonnée, des années précédentes pour revenir à une architecture commerciale plus ludique. Johnson salua l'importance documentaire du travail réalisé par Margolies sur « cette portion oubliée du magnifique patrimoine architectural américain », estimant qu'il était « sans doute le plus grand spécialiste dans ce domaine ». Un avis partagé par le critique Paul Goldberger, qui qualifia Margolies de « père de tout un mouvement ».

Margolies commença donc à attirer intérêt et encouragements, et le scandale provoqué par son exposition de 1970 pour l'Architectural League apparut vite comme un épisode de tension parmi d'autres dans une période de profonde transition. Le modernisme perdit du terrain. La crise énergétique que connut cette décennie remit en question les superautoroutes et l'idéologie de la vitesse qu'elles avaient engendrée. D'une certaine manière, les automobilistes américains furent obligés de lever le pied et de renouer avec l'esprit originel de la route.

En 1972, Robert Venturi et Denise Scott Brown publièrent leur fameux essai *L'Enseignement de Las Vegas*, dans lequel ils prirent la défense de l'aménagement des bords de route – dont l'illustration la plus pharaonique est le Strip de Las Vegas, mais qui se retrouvait aux portes de presque toutes les villes américaines, petites ou grandes – et rappelèrent que cette tradition

remontait aux premières heures de l'automobile. Tous deux étaient fascinés par l'architecture populaire reniée par les modernistes. Ils se concentrèrent sur deux catégories de cette architecture « vernaculaire » : d'un côté, les « hangars décorés » (des bâtiments de construction simple, banals, recouverts de messages publicitaires destinés à attirer l'attention des voyageurs et généralement surplombés d'une enseigne aussi criarde et voyante que possible, dans le style des casinos de Las Vegas, réputés pour leurs cascades de lumières multicolores), de l'autre, les « Canards », des établissements dont la forme physique indiquait la philosophie ou la fonction, comme les cafés en forme de tasse ou de cafetière.

Cette dernière catégorie de bâtiments « mimétiques » doit son nom au marché à la volaille de Long Island, un immense bâtiment en forme de canard logiquement baptisé The Big Duck. Ce gros volatile de béton était une attraction locale, et bien que les modernistes comme Peter Blake l'aient tourné en dérision, le grand public éprouvait pour lui une certaine tendresse, tout comme Venturi et Scott Brown.

L'Enseignement de Las Vegas soutenait que ces types d'architecture populaire représentaient une source d'inspiration iconographique et symbolique précieuse pour les « grands architectes ». Margolies alla plus loin : « Venturi et Scott Brown disaient qu'il était possible de s'inspirer de ça pour créer de vraies choses. Moi, je dis que *c'est ça* les vraies choses. »

Avec cette prise de position, Margolies s'inscrivit non seulement parmi les architectes et critiques du mouvement postmoderne naissant, mais aussi dans la vague conservatrice qui prenait son élan à cette même époque. Un groupe, appelé la « Société pour une archéologie commerciale », fut constitué en 1977 pour célébrer l'architecture de bord de route et la sauver de l'oubli et de la décrépitude. Les vieilles stations-service et les *diners* se firent bientôt enregistrer au Département des monuments historiques pour figurer sur la liste des bâtiments américains à préserver. Alors que la musique et l'art populaire américain connaissaient une seconde naissance, l'architecture de bord de route fut à nouveau prise en considération.

Les anthropologues, les historiens de la culture populaire et les architectes se mirent aussi à prêter davantage attention aux établissements routiers. En 1979, deux collègues de Venturi et Scott Brown, Paul Hirschorn et Steven Izenour, publièrent un livre intitulé *White Towers*, consacré à l'architecture d'une chaîne de hamburgers standardisée. La même année, Richard J. S. Gutman sortit son célèbre *American Diner*, le premier ouvrage entièrement dédié à l'histoire de ce type de constructions, et Warren Belasco publia *Americans on the Road : From Autocamp to Motel*, une étude du voyage automobile de 1910 à 1945. Un an plus tard, Jim Heimann présenta une riche série de bâtiments mimétiques dans *California Crazy*. En 1982, John Baeder rassembla dans *Gas, Food and Lodging* les cartes postales arborant ses peintures réalistes de *diners*. En 1985 sortit le premier ouvrage historique de référence sur l'architecture vernaculaire des routes américaines, *Main Street to Miracle Mile*.

Pendant ce temps, Margolies continua à progresser sur la scène artistique américaine et à se rapprocher du cercle de lumière. En 1978, son travail fut pour la première fois principalement financé par la Bourse Guggenheim pour la critique architecturale. Il fut ensuite subventionné à plusieurs reprises par le National Endowment for the Arts et, en 2003, la Fondation Alicia Patterson lui accorda une importante bourse en photojournalisme. Ces bourses et les dons publics ou privés qu'il reçut au fil des années lui permirent de continuer ses voyages. Il calcula un jour qu'en 1979 et 1980 il avait passé quatre mois par an, soit une nuit sur trois, dans le motel bizarroïde d'un endroit qu'il ne connaissait pas quelques heures plus tôt.

En 1980, Margolies organisa au Cooper-Hewitt National Design Museum de New York une importante exposition consacrée aux hôtels de la région montagneuse des Catskills, dans l'État de New York, parfois surnommée la « Borscht Belt ». L'année suivante, Richard Koshalek, conservateur de l'Hudson River Museum de Yonkers (État de New York), rendit hommage à son travail avec une exposition intitulée *The End of the Road*, qui présentait diverses reliques du commerce routier : une enseigne alambiquée en néon dessinant les charmants contours d'une serveuse apportant un *milk-shake*

immaculé sur fond de forêt de sapins verdoyants, un grand nombre de clichés de *drive-in* pris depuis l'arrière de l'écran, des murs ornés de fresques aux couleurs souvent passées… Toutes ces images avaient une saveur nostalgique au lendemain des années 1970, alors que ces bâtiments et attractions de bord de route commençaient à tomber en ruine.

Les images de Margolies s'affichaient donc en grand sur les murs des musées, et aussi à plat, dans plusieurs ouvrages publiés au cours de cette décennie. En 1987, il ressortit ses photos de mini-golfs pour illustrer une histoire de ce sport rédigée par Nina Garfinkel et Maria Reidelbach. L'éditeur avait eu la riche idée de réaliser la couverture en pelouse synthétique Astroturf, celle utilisée sur ces parcours. Pour *Hitting the Road – The Art of the American Road Map*, Margolies collabora avec un confrère collectionneur de cartes, Douglas A. Yorke Jr., et avec le designer Eric Baker. Sous le titre *Ticket to Paradise*, Margolies rassembla avec l'aide d'Emily Gwathmey ses photos de cinémas prises dans une multitude de petites et grandes villes américaines, les « Bijous » et autres « Odéons » de rues principales souvent délabrées et désertées. Ces livres dédiés à l'Amérique des petites villes permirent à Margolies de rappeler ces endroits à la mémoire collective et au cœur de chaque Américain.

Héritage

Le travail de Margolies, salué dans le monde entier, redonna vie à une période de l'histoire américaine autrement menacée d'extinction. Le cadrage et l'angle de vue semblent dénués d'implication émotionnelle (mais pas d'ironie), bien loin d'un plaidoyer larmoyant, pourtant ses photos ont un impact profond sur le public. Leur rectitude et leur absence de rhétorique visuelle vieillissent bien. Ces images racontent la splendeur et la décadence, sans romantisme. La présence de ces lieux n'a fait que croître, comme par magie, à mesure qu'ils partaient en poussière. Nombre de ces bâtisses n'existent plus aujourd'hui que dans ces photos qui, avec le temps, sont parvenues à incarner une réalité

propre, un paysage mythique que quelques-uns d'entre nous ont habité, mais que nous avons tous imaginé.

Grâce à la puissance de ses œuvres, Margolies rencontra un accueil enthousiaste non seulement en Amérique, mais aussi dans des recoins du monde bien éloignés de son pays natal. En 2004, il fut ainsi primé par l'Association des photographes de Macao. En 2009, à l'occasion d'une exposition organisée à Rome, la télévision italienne lui réserva un traitement digne d'une vedette de la mode.

En donnant à voir cette Amérique de légende, et grâce à son étrange capacité à toujours arriver juste avant les bulldozers, Margolies incita nombre d'observateurs à s'engager pour la préservation des bâtiments historiques.

Les archives de Margolies, tout comme sa collection d'éphémérides et d'objets, sont reconnues pour leur valeur documentaire inestimable. C. Ford Peatross, le directeur du Centre pour l'architecture, le design et l'ingénierie du Département photographie de la Bibliothèque du Congrès, fort conscient de l'importance de ses photos, entreprit de les acquérir, afin de les mettre à disposition du grand public.

Et Peatross ne fut pas le seul à convoiter ce trésor. Leanne Mella, spécialiste des arts visuels au Département d'État américain, déclara : « Les archives photographiques de John Margolies sur l'architecture routière américaine sont considérées comme l'étude la plus complète existant à ce jour sur ce sujet. » Le programme dirigé par Mella ne tarda pas à organiser une exposition consacrée à son travail, *American Roadside Architecture*, qui fit pendant plusieurs années le tour des ambassades, des consulats et d'autres institutions américaines de par le monde, afin de donner à l'étranger la vision d'une Amérique idéale, dont chaque parcelle serait aussi belle qu'un décor de film hollywoodien. Les citoyens du monde entier purent ainsi contempler la station-service en forme de soucoupe volante, les *drive-in* et « hôtels modernes » saisis par l'objectif de Margolies en Estonie, en Ukraine, à Hong Kong ou au siège de l'UNESCO à Paris. Il découvrit ainsi que les décors qu'il avait tant aimés fascinaient aussi le reste du monde.

La collection unique façonnée par Margolies fait aujourd'hui partie du domaine public, elle a rejoint les documents qui constituent l'histoire réelle des États-Unis. Dans ces images survit l'œuvre de génies quasiment tombés dans l'oubli.

Tout comme Hérodote immortalisa par les mots la vie des civilisations anciennes, Margolies consacra sa vie à recenser les images d'une culture. Il explora le défilé interminable des constructions de bord de route auquel la croissance économique et la folie de l'automobile avaient donné naissance.

L'Histoire retiendra qu'il fut un temps où une vague inégalée de créativité déferla sur un territoire presque vierge. Et que de cette terre surgit une civilisation inégalée. Dès la découverte du pétrole au Texas en 1903, puis en 1908 avec l'arrivée sur le marché de la Ford T, en quelques décennies à peine, cette civilisation goulue d'or noir a strié le continent de rubans d'asphalte et de béton. Contrairement aux paysages plus traditionnels d'Europe ou d'Asie, la plupart des bâtiments bordant les routes américaines ont été construits à la hâte pour des clients de passage, ce qui n'était pas le cas dans les paysages urbains plus traditionnels, destinés à être regardés de plus près.

Ce dialecte architectural représente une facette fondamentale de l'esprit américain. Voilà pourquoi l'œuvre de Margolies constitue un chapitre de l'histoire américaine : elle porte témoignage d'une phase cruciale de la construction de la personnalité américaine. Sans elle, comment pourrions-nous convaincre les générations futures que nous allions au *drive-in*, où des serveuses chaussées de patins à roulettes nous apportaient les repas sur des plateaux que nous accrochions aux portières, ou que nous sortions des sentiers battus pour dormir dans des tipis en béton ? Comment expliquerions-nous aux ressortissants d'autres pays que les Américains prenaient plaisir à se ranger sur des parkings géants pour regarder des films projetés sur d'immenses écrans, dont les images vacillantes étaient visibles à des kilomètres à la ronde ?

Surtout, les œuvres de John Margolies rassemblées dans cet ouvrage rendent hommage au génie et aux heureux hasards des premières heures de la culture automobile américaine.

OPPOSITE AND ABOVE Dinosaur World, Eureka Springs, Arkansas, 1994

46

RIGHT Flinstone's Bedrock City, Dinosaur Slide, Valle, Arizona, 1987

ABOVE AND OPPOSITE Flinstone's Bedrock City, Valle, Arizona, 1987

50

ABOVE Deer Acres, Pinconning, Michigan, 1988   OPPOSITE Wonder Bread Building, Rock Springs, Wyoming, 2004

MAXIE

D'S LARGEST GOOSE

SUMNER, MO.

53

OPPOSITE Maxie, World's Largest Goose, Sumner, Missouri, 1988

TOP LEFT AND RIGHT Black River Falls Oasis, Black River, Wisconsin, 1988

BOTTOM LEFT Bodin's on the Lake, Ashland, Wisconsin, 1988

BOTTOM RIGHT World's Largest Buffalo, Jamestown, North Dakota, 1980

OPPOSITE Hell Hole Ride, Steeplechase Pier, Atlantic City, New Jersey, 1978   ABOVE Gorilla Girl Sign, Atlantic City, New Jersey, 1978

OPPOSITE Xanadu Foam House of Tomorrow, Wisconsin Dells, Wisconsin, 1988   ABOVE Galaxy Four Indian Arts and Crafts, Grand Canyon, Arizona, 1987

58

ABOVE LEFT Banana Water Slide, Virginia Beach, Virginia, 1985

ABOVE RIGHT Peach Water Tower, Gaffney, South Carolina, 1988

59

ABOVE World's Largest Pecan, James Farms, Brunswick, Missouri, 1988

ABOVE Storybook Gardens, Good Ship Lollypop, Lake Delton, Wisconsin, 1988

ABOVE LEFT Magic Forest, Lake George, New York, 1996

ABOVE RIGHT Molly Brown's Fireworks, Valley Park, Missouri, 1988

62

ABOVE Marine Life, Rapid City, South Dakota, 1987   **OPPOSITE** Shell Gas Station Restoration, Winston-Salem, North Carolina, 1982

ABOVE The Hogan Indian Arts and Crafts, Mancos, Colorado, 1991   OPPOSITE 1941 Cafe, Lowell, Arkansas, 1984

ABOVE LEFT Storybrook Land Park, Aberdeen, South Dakota, 1987

ABOVE RIGHT Kelbee's Ice Cream, Winthrop, Maine, 1984

ABOVE LEFT Storybrook Land Park, Aberdeen, South Dakota, 1987

ABOVE RIGHT Mr. Peanut, Swansea, Massachusetts, 1984

PRIVATE

OPPOSITE Pirate Statue, Ocean City, Maryland, 1985   **ABOVE** The Ghost Ship, Nags Head, North Carolina, 1985

70

TOP LEFT Thunderbeast Park, Chiloquin, Oregon, 1987

BOTTOM LEFT Dinosaur Park, Rapid City, South Dakota, 1987

TOP AND BOTTOM RIGHT Dinosaur World, Eureka Springs, Arkansas, 1994

OPPOSITE Prehistoric Forest, Onsted, Michigan, 1988

OPPOSITE Big Daddy's Pawn Shop, Texarkana, Texas, 1993   ABOVE Brown's Taxidermy Studio, Camden, Arkansas, 1979

ABOVE Erie Foreign Car Parts, Whitesboro, New York, 1987   **OPPOSITE** Spindle Parking Lot Sculpture by Dustin Shuler, Berwyn, Illinois, 2003

OPPOSITE The Igloo Ice Cream, Toledo, Ohio, 1988

TOP LEFT The Matterhorn, Prairie Dell, Texas, 1982

BOTTOM LEFT Petrified Rock Park, Lemmon, South Dakota, 1987

TOP RIGHT Iceberg Gas Station, Ottawa, Kansas, 1980

BOTTOM RIGHT Iceberg Tavern, Tulsa, Oklahoma, 1979

78

ABOVE LEFT Snowman Statue, Saint Paul, Minnesota, 1984

ABOVE RIGHT Magic Forest, Lake George, New York, 1996

ABOVE Christmas Spirit, Ocean City, Maryland, 1985

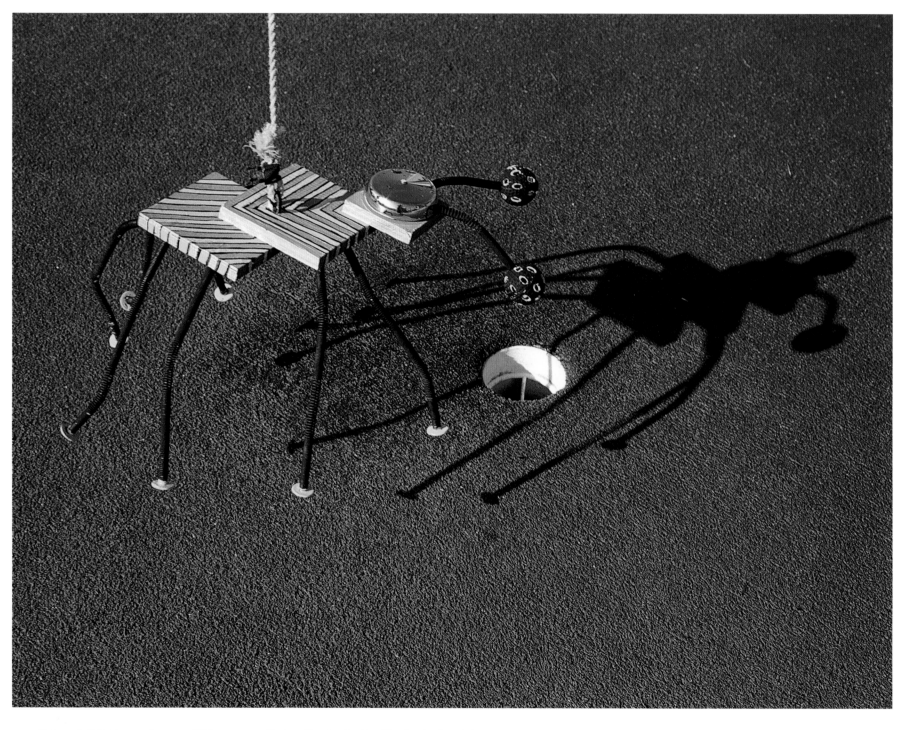

ABOVE Sir Goony Golf, Chattanooga, Tennessee, 1986   **OPPOSITE** Northrup King Corn Plot, Vermillion, South Dakota, 1987

ABOVE Aquarius Hero King Luncheonette, Titusville, Florida, 1979   **OPPOSITE** Mailbox, Saint Augustine, Florida, 1979

85

OPPOSITE Jack's Trading Center, Carlsbad, New Mexico, 1979   ABOVE Horseless Carriage Museum, Rockerville, South Dakota, 1980

2 MI.

YOU NEVER SAUSAGE A PLACE!
(YOU'RE ALWAYS A WEINER AT PEDRO'S!)

SOUTH OF THE BORDER

OPPOSITE AND ABOVE South of the Border, Dillon, South Carolina, 1985

ABOVE South Point 1 Hour Photo, Key West, Florida, 1990   **OPPOSITE** Eat It Raw Half Shell Raw Bar, Key West, Florida, 1990

90

ABOVE Manny's Alligator Center, Oak Hill, Florida, 1990   **OPPOSITE** Gatorland Zoo, Kissimmee, Florida, 1980

Gatorland Zoo KISSIMMEE ORLANDO FLA.

ABOVE El Rancho Motel, Redding, California, 1987

ABOVE LEFT Saddle & Spur Lounge, Monroe, Louisiana, 1982

ABOVE RIGHT Western Holiday Motel, Wichita, Kansas, 1993

ABOVE City Jail, Frederick, South Dakota, 1987   **OPPOSITE** A-1 Taxi, El Paso, Texas, 1982

ABOVE Jim Frey Bird Houses, Trenton, Maine, 1995

ABOVE The Monkey Junction, Wilmington, North Carolina, 1985

TOP RIGHT Capri Drive-in Theater, Marshall, Texas, 1982

BOTTOM RIGHT Texan Drive-in Theater, Pecos, Texas, 1979

TOP LEFT FT-Roc Drive-in, Rock Hill, South Carolina, 1982

OPPOSITE Rocket Drive-in Theater, Sweetwater, Texas, 1979

BOTTOM LEFT Star Lite Outdoor Theatre, Fargo, North Dakota, 1980

ABOVE Romantic Motor Vu, Craigo, Colorado, 1980

ABOVE Terrace Drive-in Theater, Bakersfield, California, 1987

OPPOSITE Southernmost Point, Key West, Florida, 1985   **ABOVE** Motel, Nickel Creek, Texas, 1993

ABOVE Bell Boy Motel Sign, Wichita, Kansas, 1979   **OPPOSITE** Bel Shore Motel Signs, Lordsburg, New Mexico, 1991

OPPOSITE Blue Mist Motel, Miami Beach, Florida, 1990   ABOVE Bon Ton Bar, Bay City, Michigan, 1982

OPPOSITE Reed's Gifts Sign, Warren, Maine, 1984   ABOVE National Freshwater Fishing Hall of Fame, Hayward, Wisconsin, 1988

ABOVE Advance Roofing Space Shuttle Sign, Mims, Florida, 1990   **OPPOSITE** Old Pro Golf, Space Course, Ocean City, Maryland, 1985

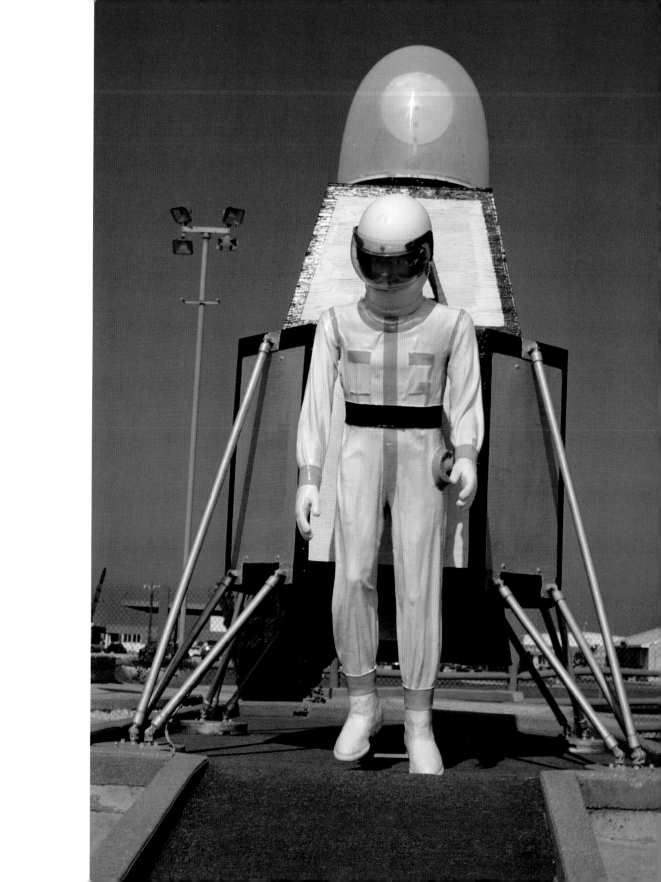

LEFT Ace Travel Service, Del Rio, Texas, 1982

ABOVE LEFT Old Pro Golf, Circus Course, Ocean City, Maryland, 1985

ABOVE RIGHT Dinosaur Gardens, Ossineke, Michigan, 1988

ABOVE Mother Goose Market, Hazard, Kentucky, 1979   **OPPOSITE** Steel's Country Kitchen Sign, Pensacola, Florida, 1979

LEFT Totem Pole Park, Foyil, Oklahoma, 2001

ABOVE LEFT Chieftan Motel Statue, Carrington, North Dakota, 1987

ABOVE RIGHT Herb Drew's Plumbing and Heating, Danville, Illinois, 1983

OPPOSITE Big Indian Shop, Shelburne Falls, Massachusetts, 1995

ABOVE LEFT Traveler's Chapel, Alexandria, Louisiana, 1979

ABOVE CENTER Roadside Teepee, Sitting Bull's Crystal Cave, Rapid City, South Dakota, 1980

ABOVE RIGHT Geronimo's Castle Tavern, Bowie, Arizona, 1979

121

ABOVE Indian Trading Post, Elk City, Oklahoma, 1982

ABOVE LEFT Big Indian Shop, Mohawk Teepee Statue, Shelburne Falls, Massachusetts, 1996

ABOVE RIGHT Casco Bay Trading Post, Chief Passamaquoddy Statue, Freeport, Maine, 1984

ABOVE Pocahontas Gifts, Pocahontas, Iowa, 1987

124

RIGHT Indian City, Allentown, Arizona, 1979

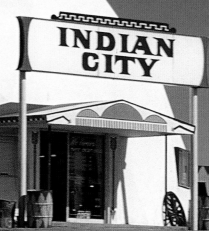

ABOVE Old Jail Billboard, Saint Augustine, Florida, 1979   **OPPOSITE** Old Jail, Saint Augustine, Florida, 1990

ABOVE LEFT Black River Falls Oasis, Black River Falls, Wisconsin, 1988

ABOVE RIGHT Fennimore Cheese Shop, Fennimore, Wisconsin, 2003

ABOVE The Cheese House, Trenton, Maine, 1985

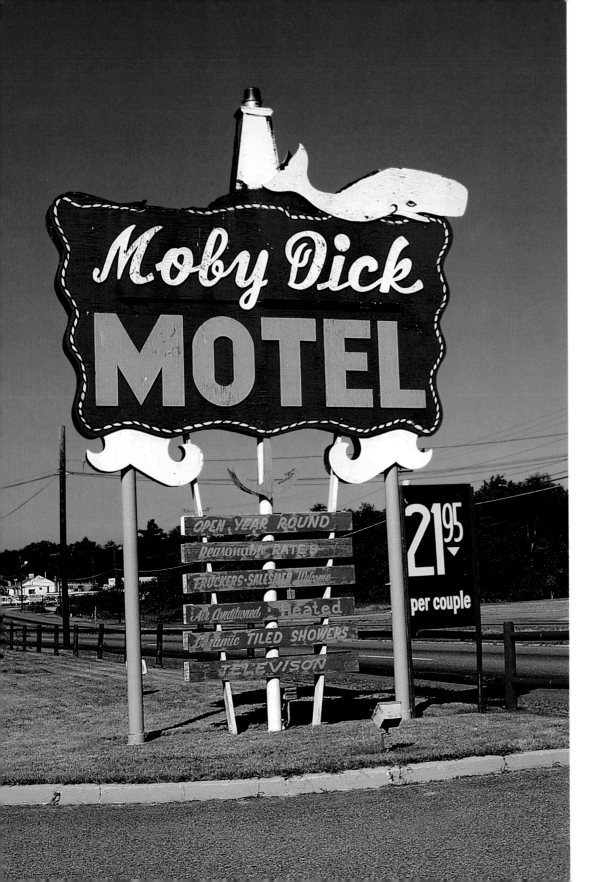

131

OPPOSITE Moby Dick Motel Sign, Dartmouth, Massachusetts, 1984   ABOVE Yoken's Restaurant Sign, Portsmouth, New Hampshire, 1984

TOP RIGHT Surf Slide Shark Statue, Nags Head, North Carolina, 1985

BOTTOM RIGHT Jockey's Ridge Mini-Golf, Nags Head, North Carolina, 1985

OPPOSITE Magic Carpet Golf, Key West, Florida, 1985

TOP LEFT Gaido's Restaurant Sign, Galveston, Texas, 1986

BOTTOM LEFT Fenton's Seafood Market, Trenton, Maine, 1984

OPPOSITE AND ABOVE Putter's Paradise Miniature Golf, West Yarmouth, Massachusetts, 1984

Log Cabin MOTEL

LOW RATES

VACANCY

SORRY

OPPOSITE Log Cabin Motel Sign, Montrose, Colorado, 1991

TOP LEFT Red Run Lodge, Rouzerville, Pennsylvania, 1982

TOP RIGHT Louie's Cabin, Laurel, Montana, 1980

BOTTOM LEFT Saint Regis Camp Cabin, Saint Regis, Montana, 1987

BOTTOM RIGHT Log Cabin Motel Sign, Salina, Kansas, 1996

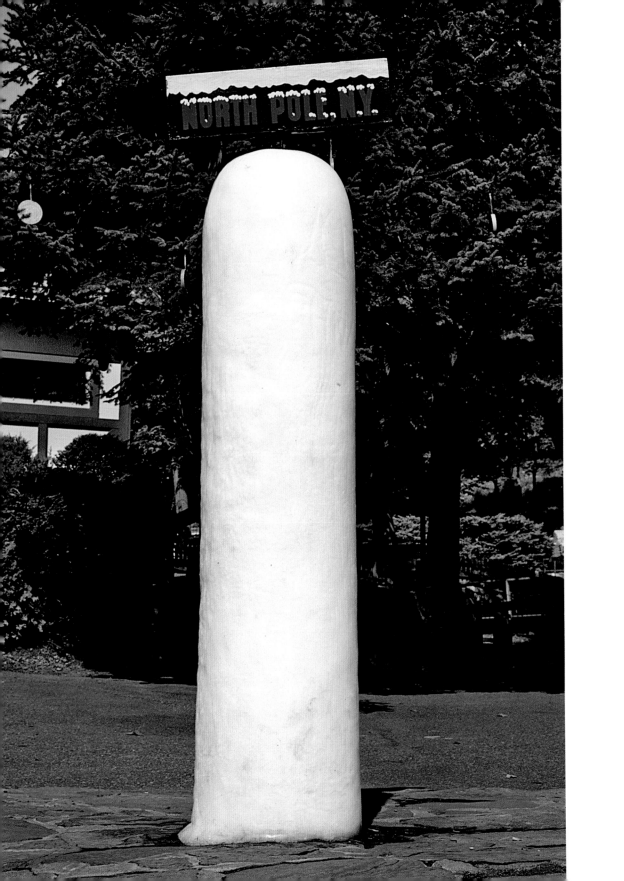

139

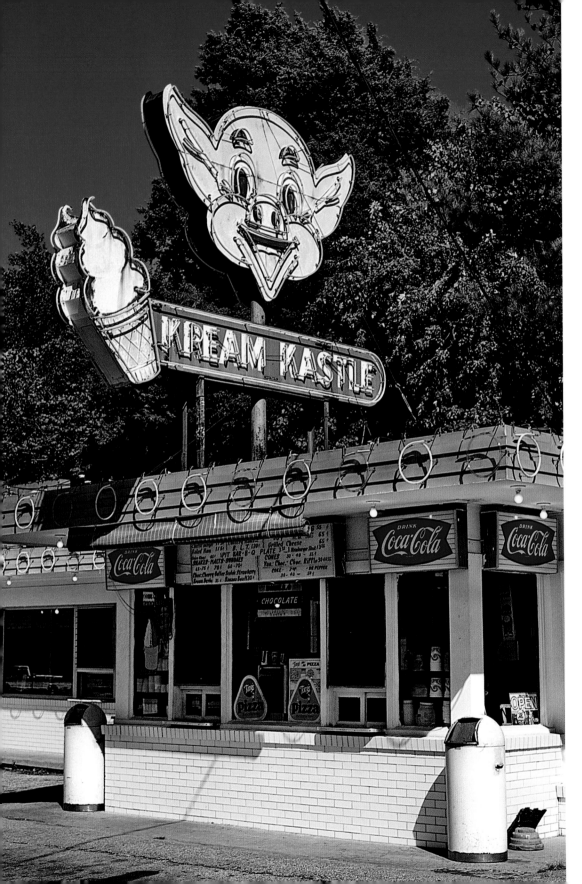

LEFT Kream Kastle, Brownsville, Tennessee, 1979

OPPOSITE Pig Stand, San Antonio, Texas, 1982

RIGHT Wigwam Village Motel #2, Cave City, Kentucky, 1979

145

LEFT D-C 7 Steakhouse, Byron, Georgia, 1982

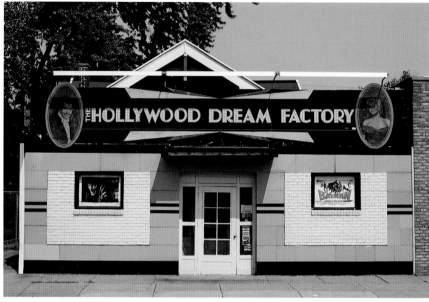

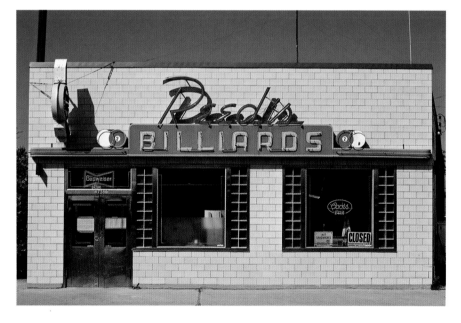

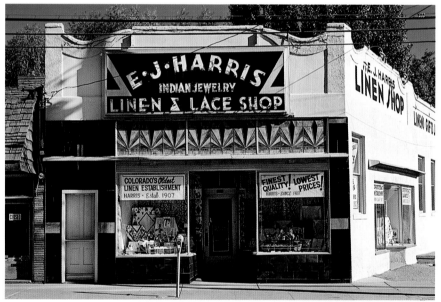

TOP LEFT Jamaican Joe's Tattoo Studio, Jacksonville, North Carolina, 1985

BOTTOM LEFT Reed's Billiards, Provo, Utah, 1980

TOP RIGHT Hollywood Dream Factory Video Store, Toledo, Ohio, 1988

BOTTOM RIGHT Harris Linen & Lace Shop, Manitou Springs, Colorado, 1980

ABOVE Spot Cleaners, Seattle, Washington, 1980

149

OPPOSITE Rawhide City Billboard, Mandan, North Dakota, 1980   ABOVE Big John, El Dorado, Illinois, 1993

ABOVE Newcastle Motel, Virginia Beach, Virginia, 1985   OPPOSITE Broiler Cafe, Salt Lake City, Utah, 1980

OPPOSITE Bull Bar Sign, Key West, Florida, 1985   **ABOVE** Bank of Rhame, Rhame, North Dakota, 1987

155

OPPOSITE Savage Theater, Booneville, Arkansas, 1979

ABOVE LEFT Cosmopolitan Theater, El Paso, Texas, 1979   **ABOVE CENTER** Lakewood Theater, Dallas, Texas, 1994   **ABOVE RIGHT** 5th Avenue Theater, Inglewood, California, 1976

ABOVE Crim Theater, Kilgore, Texas, 1982

ABOVE Gem Theater, Claude, Texas, 1982

158

ABOVE LEFT Jewel Box, Bristol, Virginia, 1979

ABOVE RIGHT Winn-Dixie Super Market, Jacksonville, Florida, 1979

ABOVE Dakota Theater, Yankton, South Dakota, 1987

ABOVE Hunt's Casino, Wildwood, New Jersey, 1978   OPPOSITE Interwestern Bus Depot, Great Falls, Montana, 1987

OPPOSITE Egyptian Theater, DeKalb, Illinois, 1979   ABOVE Martin Theater, Panama City, Florida, 1979

Martin
BLDG FOR SALE
STARRING
PORTER DEESE DEESE REALTY
BLDG FOR SALE
STARRING
PORTER DEESE DEESE REALTY

OPPOSITE Martin Theater, Talladega, Alabama, 1980

ABOVE LEFT Roxy Theater Ticket Booth, Caldwell, Ohio, 1977   ABOVE CENTER Crest Theater Ticket Booth, Fresno, California, 1987   ABOVE RIGHT State Theater Ticket Booth, Deposit, New York, 1977

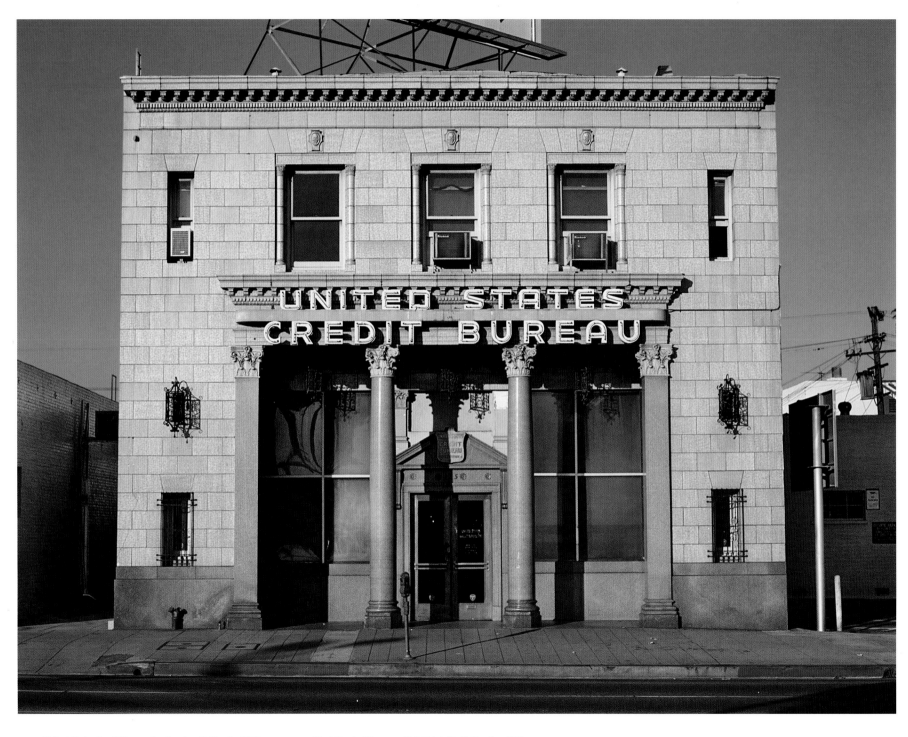

ABOVE United States Credit Bureau, Los Angeles, California, 1985   **OPPOSITE** Giant Chest of Drawers, High Point, North Carolina, 2001

ABOVE Cuban Liquors, Baton Rouge, Louisiana, 1982   **OPPOSITE** Carvel Ice Cream Sign, West Haverstraw, New York, 1980

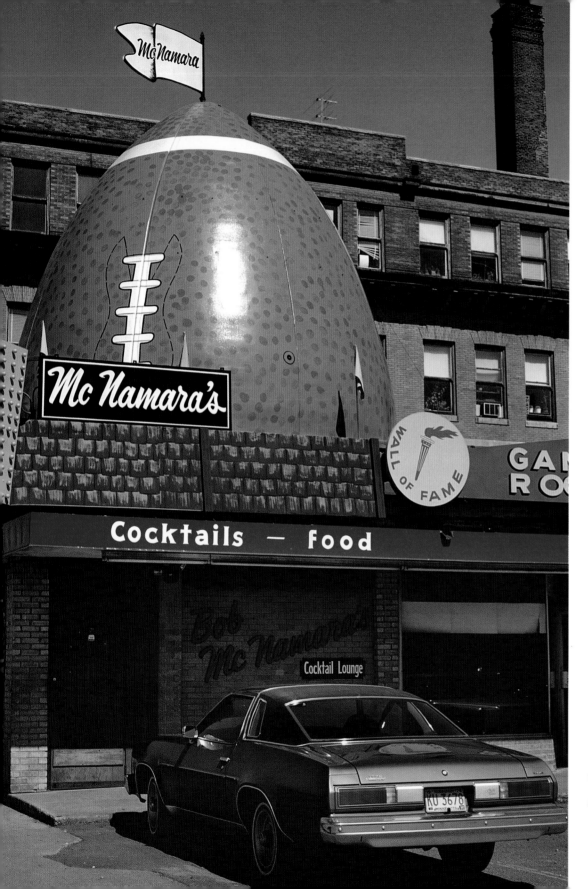

LEFT McNamara's Tavern, Minneapolis, Minnesota, 1977

OPPOSITE Rivers Edge Realty, Savage, Minnesota, 1983

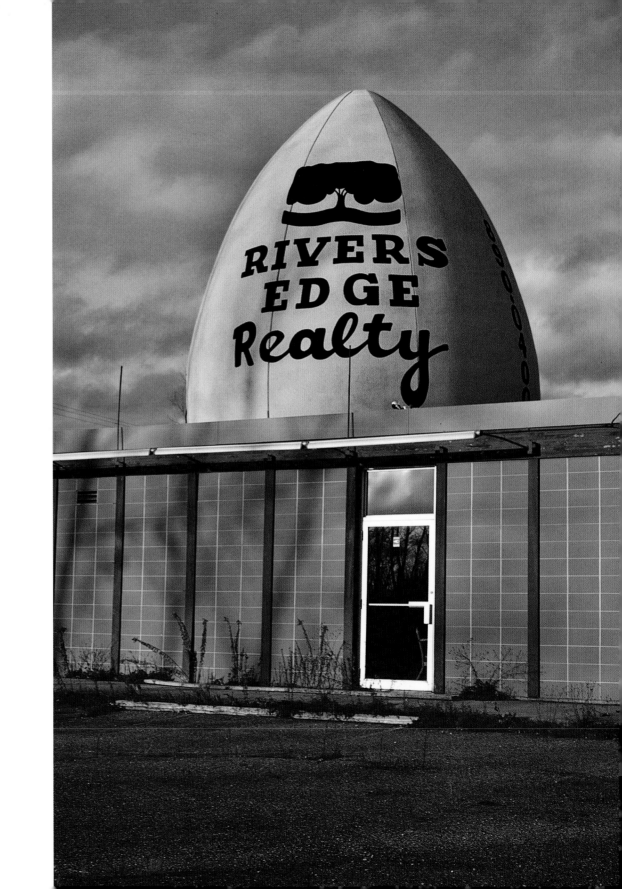

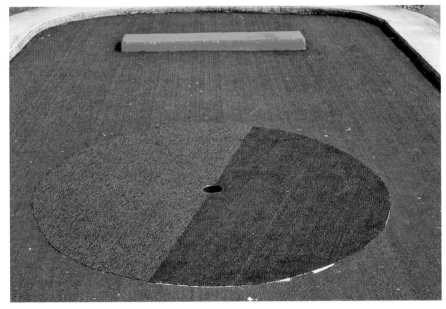

OPPOSITE Hole in One Miniature Golf, Waldoboro, Maine, 1984

TOP LEFT Cerri's Mini Golf, Marcy, New York, 1987

BOTTOM LEFT Castle Park Golf, Fort Lauderdale, Florida, 1985

TOP RIGHT Around the World in 18 Holes, Lake Placid, New York, 2002

BOTTOM RIGHT Queen Pines Mini Golf, Redding, California, 1987

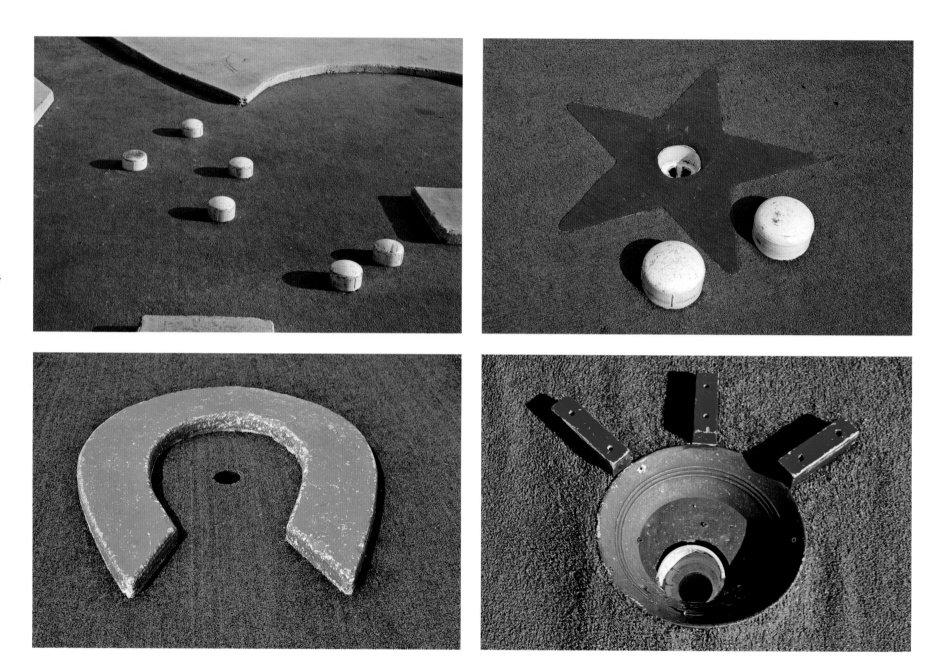

174

TOP LEFT AND RIGHT Blackbeard's Mini Golf, Fresno, California, 1987

BOTTOM LEFT Castle Park Golf, Fort Lauderdale, Florida, 1985

BOTTOM RIGHT Flags of Fun Amusement Park, Rapid City, South Dakota, 1987

ABOVE Jawor's Fun Golf, Roseville, Michigan, 1986

OPPOSITE Mauro's Mini Golf, Hazel Park, Michigan, 1986

TOP LEFT Holiday Golf, Daytona Shores, Florida, 1985

BOTTOM LEFT Sir Goony Golf at Spring Lake Recreation Center, Chadds Ford, Pennsylvania, 1984

TOP RIGHT Jawor's Fun Golf, Roseville, Michigan, 1986

BOTTOM RIGHT Magic Carpet Golf, Key West, Florida, 1985

ABOVE Magic Carpet Golf, Key West, Florida, 1985   **OPPOSITE** Sir Goony Golf, Chattanooga, Tennessee, 1986

OPPOSITE Joyland Golf, Daytona Beach, Florida, 1990   ABOVE Harry's Kurio Kastle, Arnolds Park, Iowa, 1988

ABOVE Xpo Adult Theatre, Wilmington, California, 1976   **OPPOSITE** Stan the Tire Man, Mount Vernon, Illinois, 1988

184

ABOVE Joe's Service Garage, Nashwauk, Minnesota, 1980

OPPOSITE Broadway Style House, Shreveport, Louisiana, 1982　　ABOVE Tropics Lounge, Wichita, Kansas, 1979

R. F. RINGROSE M.D.

ABOVE LEFT China Nite Restaurant, Ogden, Utah, 1980   **ABOVE CENTER** Chew Den Sign, Roswell, New Mexico, 1979   **ABOVE RIGHT** Mark You Restaurant, Fall River, Massachusetts, 1976

ABOVE Golden City Restaurant, Columbus, Ohio, 1984

ABOVE Gas-N-Go, Ashtabula, Ohio, 1980

ABOVE Save Way Gas, Amarillo, Texas, 1976

194

ABOVE Missile Motel Sign, Oxnard, California, 1981

ABOVE LEFT Rocket Motel Sign, Joplin, Missouri, 1979

ABOVE RIGHT Super Sonic Car Wash, Billings, Montana, 1980

CHOP
SUEY

Uranium
CAFE

CHINESE & AMERICAN
FOODS

PARKING ➤

OPPOSITE Uranium Cafe, Grants, New Mexico, 1979   ABOVE Atomic Bar Sign, El Paso, Texas, 1979

200

PREVIOUS SPREAD House of Mexico Restaurant Sign, Beaumont, Texas, 1979   ABOVE Las Maracas Restaurant, South of the Border, Dillon, South Carolina, 1986   OPPOSITE South Federal Inn Sign, Riverton, Wyoming, 2004

LEFT Heinie's Steak House Sign, Springdale, Arkansas, 1984

OPPOSITE Fairway Golf, Saint Paul, Minnesota, 1984

ABOVE Wacky Golf, Myrtle Beach, South Carolina, 1988   **OPPOSITE** Allen Canning Company, Springdale, Arkansas, 1984

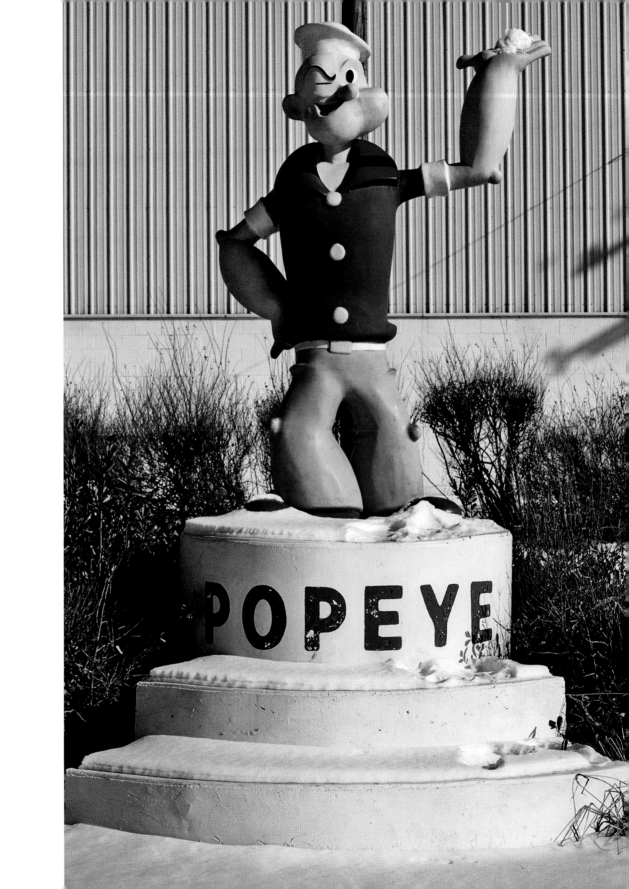

R. Lopez
the Wounded Armadillo
CLUB
HAPPY HOUR
2 TIL 7
SNACKS SERVED

OPPOSITE The Wounded Armadillo Club Sign, Richmond, Texas, 1983   ABOVE Parade Float at Liquor Mart, San Antonio, Texas, 1982

OPPOSITE DJ's Bar, Dickinson, North Dakota, 1987   ABOVE The Sleep Shop, Baton Rouge, Louisiana, 1982

ABOVE Thunderbird Drive-in Theater, Corpus Christi, Texas, 1988   **OPPOSITE** Airway Drive-in Theater Sign, Saint Ann, Missouri, 1988

AIRWAY

DRIVE IN

OPPOSITE Decker Drive-in Theater, Decker Drive, Baytown, Texas, 1979   **ABOVE** Trail Drive-in Theater Sign, Sarasota, Florida, 1980

214

ABOVE Tri City Drive-in Theatre, Loma Linda, California, 1978   OPPOSITE San Pedro Drive-in Theatre, San Pedro, California, 1979

OPPOSITE Compton Drive-in Theatre, Compton, California, 1981   ABOVE Lakewood Drive-In Theater, Lakewood, California, 1981

218

ABOVE Beltline Drive-in Theatre, Grand Rapids, Michigan, 1982

ABOVE Decker Drive-in Theatre, Baytown, Texas, 1979

220

ABOVE Town Pride Drive-in, Milwaukee, Wisconsin, 1978   OPPOSITE Tejon Theater, Bakersfield, California, 2003

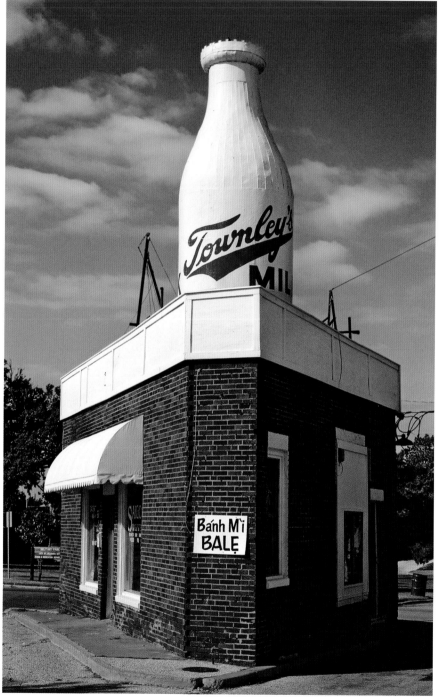

ABOVE LEFT Benewah Dairy, Spokane, Washington, 1980

ABOVE RIGHT Townley's Milk, Oklahoma City, Oklahoma, 1993

RIGHT Chatty Belle at Cheese and Gift Shop, Neillsville, Wisconsin, 1988

224

ABOVE Miner's Hat Realty, Kellogg, Idaho, 1987

ABOVE Fire Chief Hat Dog, Barstow, California, 1979

ABOVE LEFT OJ's Ice Cream Sign, Concord, New Hampshire, 1978

ABOVE RIGHT Ice Cream Sign, Quechee, Vermont, 1984

ABOVE Besto Ice Cream Sign, Anderson, South Carolina, 1988

228

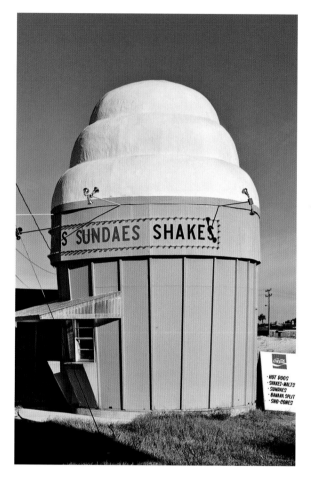

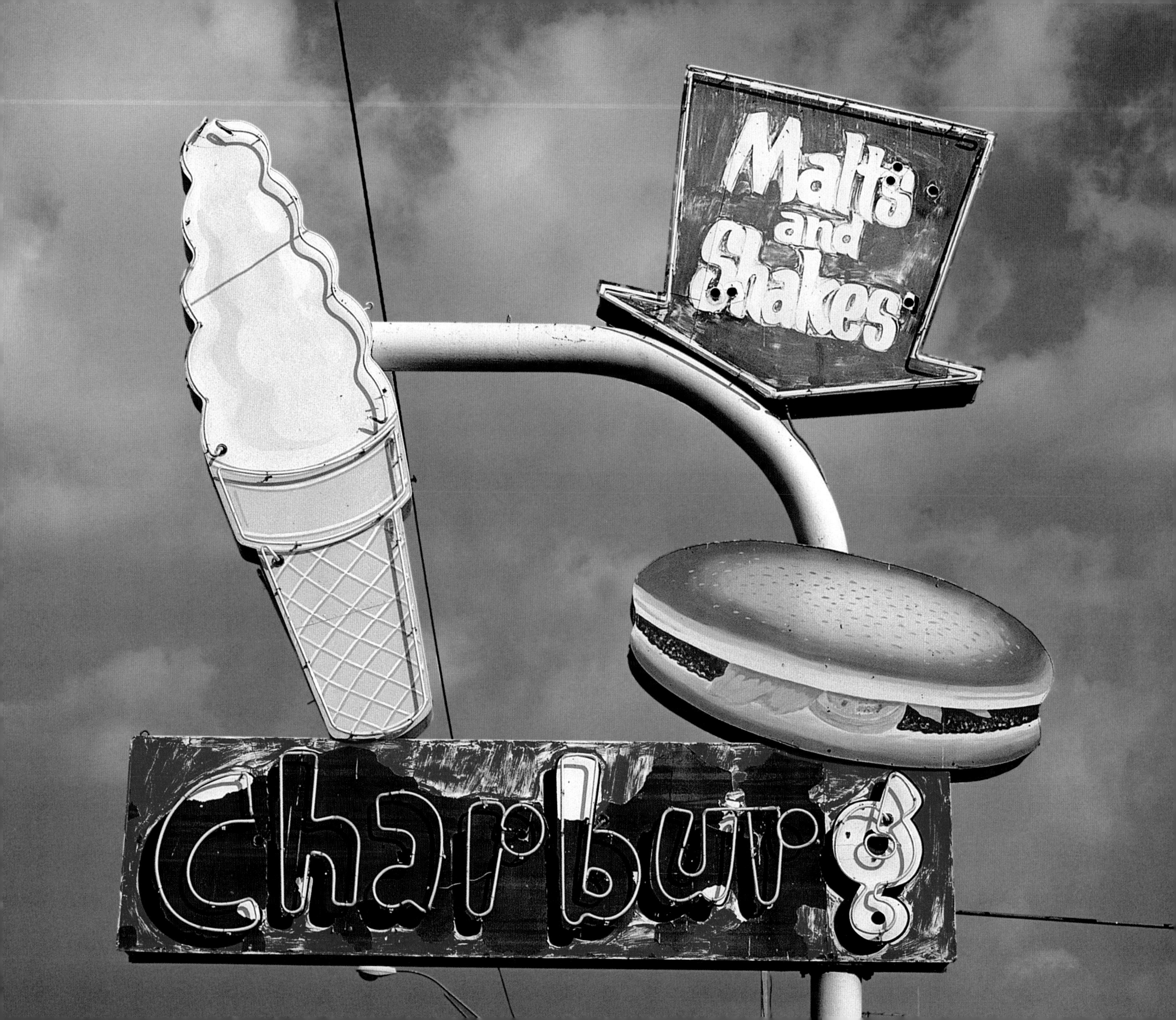
Malts and Shakes
Charburg

ABOVE Coffee Pot Tavern, Bedford, Pennsylvania, 1984

ABOVE Beef Burger, Amarillo, Texas, 1982

LEFT Leaning Tower of Niles YMCA, Niles, Illinois, 2003

ABOVE LEFT Tower of Pizza, Green Brook, New Jersey, 1978

ABOVE RIGHT Prince Restaurant, Saugus, Massachusetts, 1984

234

ABOVE Chris Shoe Repair, Springfield, Ohio, 1980

ABOVE Pat's Shoe Repair, Hiawatha, Kansas, 1988

ABOVE Coney Island Dairyland, Aspen Park, Colorado, 1980   **OPPOSITE** The Donut Hole, La Puente, California, 1991

ABOVE Sir Goony Golf, Rehoboth Beach, Delaware, 1985

ABOVE Sir Goony Golf, Chattanooga, Tennessee, 1986

240

ABOVE Texaco (Formerly Wadhams) Gas Station, Cedarburg, Wisconsin, 1977   OPPOSITE Jimmy Woo's Pagoda, Eau Claire, Wisconsin, 1980

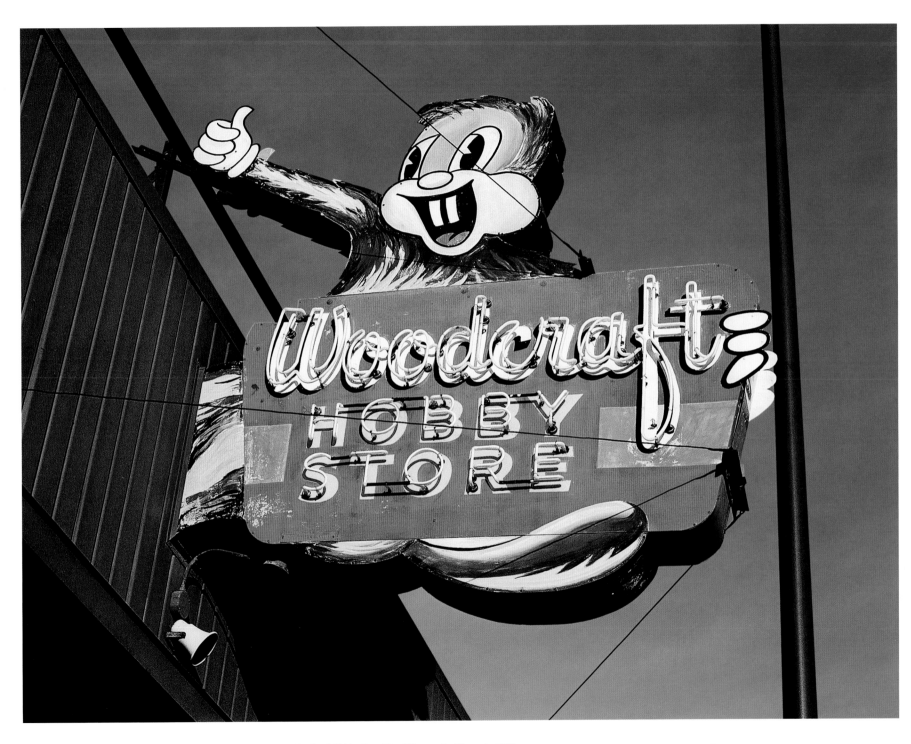

OPPOSITE Pussy Cat Lounge Sign, Fargo, North Dakota, 1980   ABOVE Woodcraft Hobby Store Sign, Minneapolis, Minnesota, 1984

244

ABOVE LEFT Valleybrook Mini Golf, Chadds Ford, Pennsylvania, 1984

ABOVE RIGHT Federal Heating and Air Conditioning, Denver, Colorado, 2004

ABOVE Little Dixie Fireworks Stand, West Monroe, Louisiana, 1982

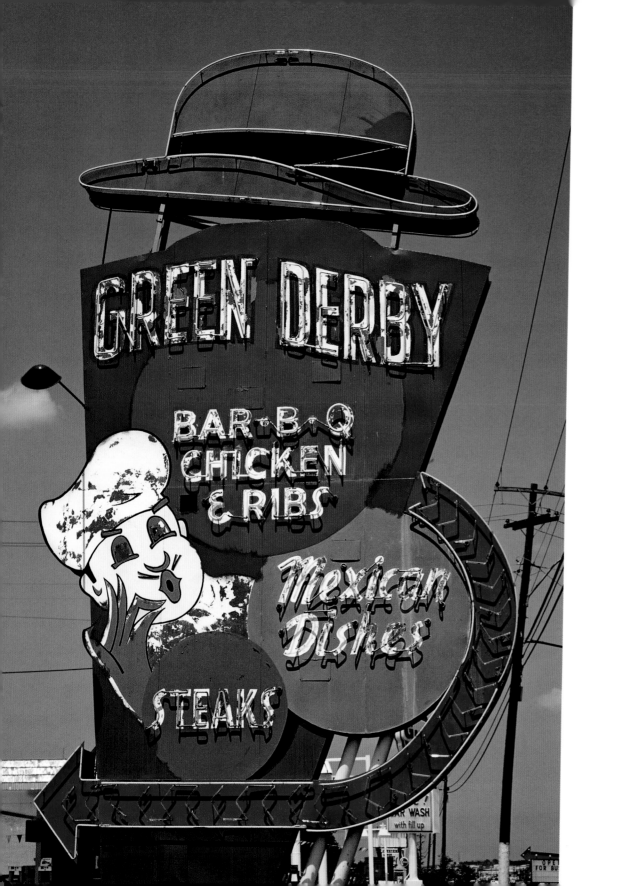

OPPOSITE Harbor Island Spa, Long Branch, New Jersey, 1978   ABOVE Aquarium, Provincetown, Massachusetts, 1984   FOLLOWING PAGE Stamie's Beachwear Jantzen Sign, Daytona Beach, Florida, 1990

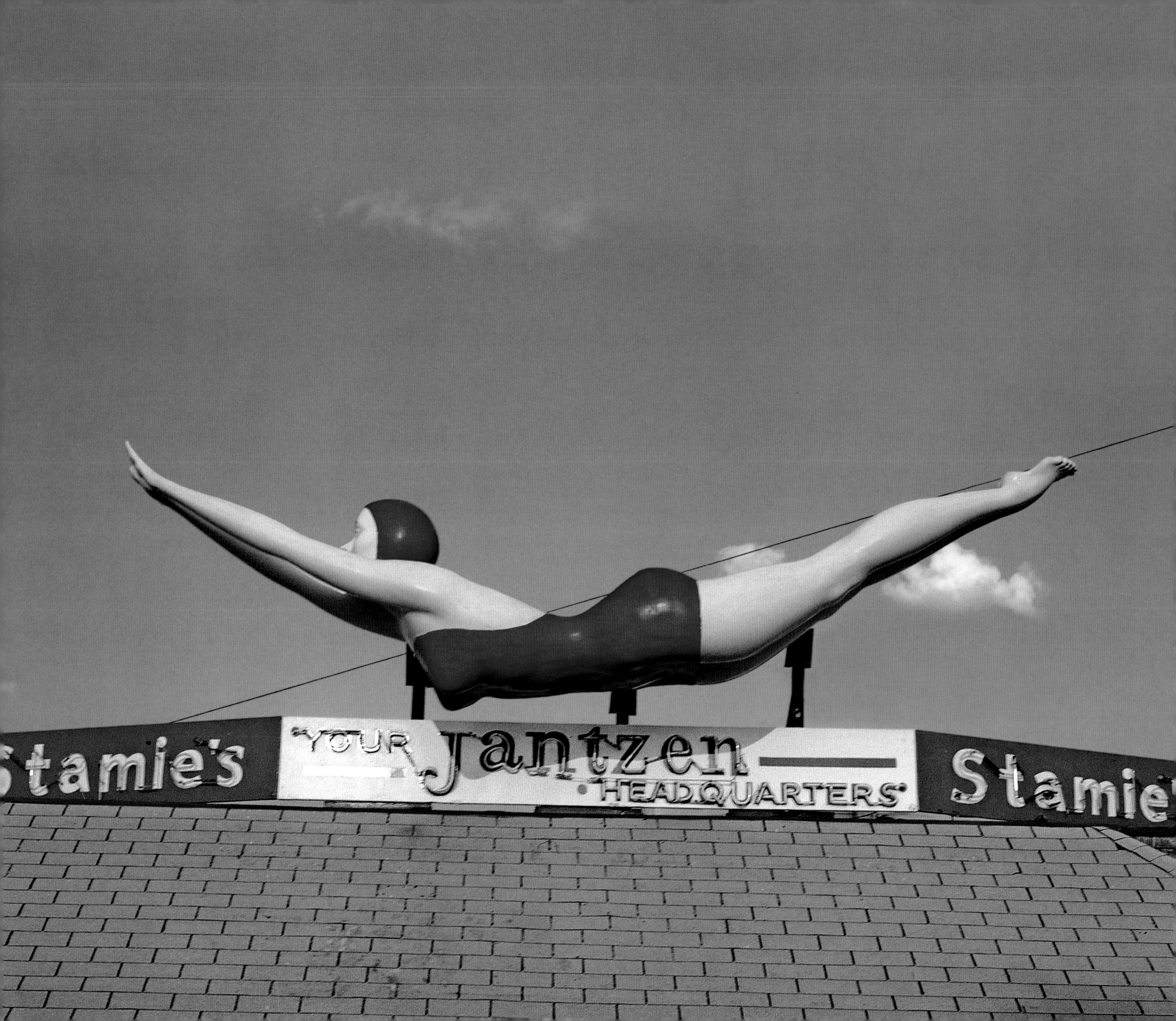
Stamie's
"YOUR Jantzen
HEADQUARTERS"
Stamie'

INDEX

Acknowledgments

254

To the many people at TASCHEN America who helped to make this book possible: Benedikt Taschen, who visited me in New York and was impressed by my archive; my editor, Jim Heimann, himself a distinguished roadside scholar, who suggested that Mr. Taschen pay me a visit and who then came east for two days to select possible images for inclusion in this book; managing editor Nina Wiener; editor Victoria Birch; art director Josh Baker; designer Marco Zivny; and interns Mallory Farrugia, Ryann McQuilton, and Katie Stahnke.

To Phil Patton for his perceptive essay, and to C. Ford Peatross for his vision and his excellent foreword.

To the funding organizations that helped to underwrite my research: The Alicia Patterson Foundation; Architectural League of New York; John Simon Guggenheim Memorial Foundation; Design Arts and Visual Arts Programs of the National Endowment for the Arts in Washington, D.C., a federal agency; New York Foundation for the Arts; and the Wyeth Endowment for American Art.

To individuals who helped with funding and with moral support: Billy Adler, Harriet Moyer Apteker, Tom Bailey, Tom Bosworth, Wendy Burton Brouws, Joanne Leonhardt Cassullo, Dave Cole, John Dunning, Tim Dye, Peggy Engel, Rosalie Genevro, Marshall Gettys, Howard Gilman, Toni Greenberg, Agnes Gund, Ellen Harris, Michael Jackson, Barbara Jakobson, Philip Johnson, Rick Landau, Chip Lord, Linda Mullestein, Carolyn Marsh, Tom Martinson, Jim Masson, Jim McClure, Tom McCue, Robert Murdock, Susan W. Paine, Leland and Crystal Payton, Christina Petoski, Susan Plum, Harold Ramis, Stephen Resnick, Cindy Rose, Susan Scranton, Karen Shatzkin, Natalie Shivers, Peter Sidlow, Erica Stoller, Nancy Stout, Jane S. Tai, Fred and Barbara Volkmann, Joan Warburg, Howard Weinberg, Daniel Wolf, and Virginia and Bagley Wright.

COVER Big Fish Supper Club, Bena, Minnesota, 1980

PREVIOUS PAGE AND BACK COVER John Margolies photographing
American Kleaner, Bakersfield, California, 2003

To stay informed about upcoming TASCHEN titles, please
request our magazine at www.taschen.com/magazine or
write to TASCHEN, Hohenzollernring 53, D-50672 Cologne,
Germany, contact@taschen.com, Fax: +49-221-254919.
We will be happy to send you a free copy of our magazine
which is filled with information about all of our books.

© 2011 TASCHEN GmbH
Hohenzollernring 53, D-50672 Köln, Germany
www.taschen.com

The publisher gratefully acknowledges the use of photographs from
the following collections: 225 and back cover: Felix Adamo/Bakersfield
Californian. 39: Collection Center for Creative Photography, University
of Arizona © 1998 Arizona Board of Regents. 16: Edward Weston Archive,
Center for Creative Photography © 1981 Arizona Board of Regents
(Posthumous digital reproduction from original negative). 11, 14, 22,
26: Jim Heimann Collection. 6, 12, 13, 23, 28, 30, 34, 36, 37: Library
of Congress, Prints & Photographs Division, FSA-OWI Collection.

Editor: Jim Heimann, Los Angeles
Art director: Josh Baker, Los Angeles
Design: Marco Zivny, Los Angeles
Editorial coordination: Victoria Birch and Nina Wiener,
   Los Angeles, and Mischa Gayring, Cologne
Production: Jennifer Patrick, Los Angeles
German translation: Anke Burger, Berlin
French translation: Alice Pétillot, Paris

Printed in China

ISBN 978-9-0000-3618-9

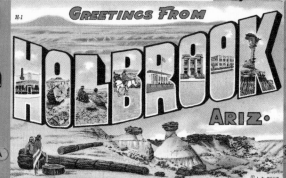